160 688937 2

D0489403

International Parental Child

International Parental Child Abduction

Authors   Anne-Marie Hutchinson

                 Henry Setright, *Barrister*

Primary researcher   Rachel Roberts of *reunite*
                       International Child Abduction Centre

 **Family Law**
1998

Published by Family Law
an imprint of Jordan Publishing Limited
21 St Thomas Street
Bristol BS1 6JS

British Library Cataloguing-in-Publication Data
A catalogue record for this book is available from the British Library.

ISBN 0 85308 466 1

Typeset by Mendip Communications Ltd, Frome, Somerset
Printed by MPG Books Ltd, Bodmin, Cornwall

Acknowledgements

This book is the culmination of a successful two-year research project undertaken by *reunite* National Council for Abducted Children, now *reunite* International Child Abduction Centre. This work has been exclusively funded by a grant from the Nuffield Foundation.

reunite, the authors and publishers of this book gratefully acknowledge and thank the following organisations and individuals for contributing their time and expertise so generously and for their continued support of *reunite*'s work and the research project:

Prof Dr IUR Albert Bach; Carol Bruch, Margaret Casey, Roberta Ceschini, Vèronique Chauveau, Stephen Crane, William Cross, Markanza Cudby, Justin Dillon, Jason Doumbis, Professor William Duncan, Andrea Dye (LCD), Ian Edge, Edwin Freeman, Ray Finnucane, Essie Grives, Ken Gumbley, Catherine Fooks, Angels Fuentes, Lawrence Hayes, Adv Barbar Hecter (Pretoria), Frederic Renstrom, George Jamieson, Zubair Khaled, Christopher Lee, Annelise Lemche, John Lloyd, Judy Lown-Golding, Anil Malhotra (India), Ranjit Malhotra (India), Katrin Saage-Fain, David Truex, Tracey Turnball, Belinda Van Heerden (University of Cape Town), Jutta Wagner (Berlin), Jeffrey Wilson, the Foreign and Commonwealth Office, the Lord Chancellor's Department, the National Center for Missing and Exploited Children USA, the Department of State USA, and the Nuffield Foundation.

Foreword
by The Rt Hon Lord Justice Ward

Wrongful removal and retention of children away from their habitual residence brings nothing in its wake but misery for all concerned, especially and inevitably, for the children. Ease of air travel, demands of employment, broadening horizons and the fragility of personal relationships lead to an ever-increasing movement of children across international boundaries. Those affected deserve immediate advice and, as importantly, well-informed advice. That expertise is provided by the authors of this much needed publication.

Henry Setright, barrister, commands the judges' respect for the dependable knowledge and skill he brings to every case in which he appears – and he has appeared in many of the most important ones.

Anne-Marie Hutchinson, solicitor and Chairperson of *reunite*, uniquely combines a detailed understanding of the procedures with an insight into the devastating effect of abduction which only *reunite* can gather.

They realise the need to have speedy access not to the minutiae but the broad outline of the many systems of law operating in the jurisdictions from which or to which the children have been taken. With the generous support of the Nuffield Foundation, *reunite* were able to research and gather that vital information and now make it available to all of us in this excellent and invaluable work.

No family lawyer in the United Kingdom should be without a copy. Indeed, since it is a truly international work it should find its place on book shelves across the world.

Due to the generosity of the authors and their collaborators, all royalties will go to *reunite*, than which is no worthier cause to support.

I commend *reunite*. I commend the book. I urge you to buy it.

SIR ALAN WARD
October 1998

Foreword

by Adair Dyer, formerly First Secretary of the Permanent Bureau of the Hague Conference on Private International Law

reunite International Child Abduction Centre has long played a leading role both in consciousness-raising and in assisting concretely with the acute family problems which fall under the rubric 'international child abduction'. It is the model for non-governmental associations, which through their initiatives provide an indispensable complement to the action taken by governments to protect children from this often very painful and destructive form of child abuse.

The publication of the *Reunite Practical Guide on Child Abduction* is a natural and most welcome extension of this organisation's prior activities in sponsoring seminars, as well as responding to individual requests for information and help. It should go a long way towards furthering the efforts of *reunite* to combat parental child abduction.

The Hague Convention on the Civil Aspects of International Child Abduction, which has set the tone for governmental efforts to combat child abduction, passed the signal marker of 50 States Parties on 1 March 1998. The governmental network is growing but the resources of the public sector are not sufficient to carry out the task alone. It is in this context that the example set by *reunite* should be seen. In the end, it will require awareness and vigilance on the part of the private sector in order to shape individual behaviour which will promote the interests of the children and families, rather than the egotistical needs of individual parents who claim that the abrupt uprooting of the child is in the child's best interests.

Article 11 of the United Nations Convention on the Rights of the Child commits its States Parties to: 'take measures to combat the illicit transfer and non-return of the children abroad'. This principle is foreshadowed by the provision in Article 10 of this treaty granting to a: 'child whose parents reside in different States ... the right to maintain on a regular basis, save in exceptional circumstances personal relations and direct contacts with both parents'. International child abduction violates this right of a child. As its name indicates, *reunite* serves to protect this fundamental right of children and families.

ADAIR DYER
October 1998

How to Use this Book

International Parental Child Abduction is a compendium of legal and practical information designed to assist practitioners and advisers in international abduction cases. The book does not set out to be an academic, theoretical textbook, but rather to draw together in sufficient detail for practical purposes the legal and procedural information necessary to make informed decisions about the treatment of abduction cases in other jurisdictions.

The book comprises two distinctive and complementary parts. Part 1 is a succinct explanation of the Conventions on child abudction and their practical application. The Part also provides an overview of the increasingly important subject of Islamic family law. The roles of the various organis-ations concerned with the resolution of abduction cases are also explained. The Part concludes by reproducing the Hague and European Conventions and provides a list of the current signatories to each.

Part 2 constitutes an alphabetically arranged country-by-country guide to dozens of different jurisdictions. Each guide contains a summary of domestic family and child law and, if it is a signatory to either jurisdiction, a summary too of the application of Convention law and practice within the jurisdiction. Wherever possible, contact details have been included.

The selection of countries covered by the book is based on the caseload of *reunite*. The countries included are those with which *reunite* has most frequently been concerned.

To avoid confusion between the different legal concepts found in different jurisdictions, many special terms are set out in the original language, in italics. A literal translation is also given. While this may not always result in the most elegant of English phraseology, it serves to highlight the fact that a specific foreign legal concept is being referred to which may differ significantly from the meaning attached to the more usual English term.

Finally, while the contributions may be taken as a guide to national procedures, they are no substitute for appropriate professional advice when acting in specific circumstances.

Contents

Part I

PART

1

International child abduction

INTRODUCTION

When a child is taken away without consent or lawful authority from a person who has the right in law to care for him or her, that child has been abducted. When a child is removed across an international frontier either having been taken from the care of such a person, or having been removed without such a person's knowledge or consent, that is an international child abduction. The term can include cases where a child is removed without the consent of a person who has the right to have a say where the child lives but who is not a physical custodian. It can also include cases where a child is retained in a foreign country contrary to the rights of another person.

Inevitably, when a child has been abducted internationally, the rights of the person from whom the child has been abducted cannot usually be effectively enforced in his or her home State. Any effective remedy must be pursued in the country in which the child is physically present. It is the diversity of laws and legal systems that such a situation produces that has given an impetus to the formulation of international conventions in child abduction.

Those countries which are signatories to one of the relevant international Conventions on child abduction are described in this work as 'Convention countries'. Those outside the Convention are described as 'non-Convention countries' where arrangements may exist which facilitate applications for the return of children but these will stem either from the existing system of law in the State in which the child is physically present, following the abduction, or from a special bilateral treaty.

INTERNATIONAL CONVENTIONS ON CHILD ABDUCTION

There are two Conventions currently operating between contracting States which are applicable to cases of international child abduction. They are the Hague Convention on the Civil Aspects of International Child Abduction ('the Hague Convention') and the European Convention on Recognition of Children ('the European Convention'). These Conventions are distinct in their approach to the practical problem of dealing with the situation of children who have been abducted internationally. Both, however, are designed to facilitate a summary and speedy process, to minimise the need for foreign law to be proved or investigated, and to provide basic and limited defences where a return would place a child's welfare at serious risk. Neither convention is concerned with the criminal aspects of child abduction.

THE HAGUE CONVENTION

THE OBJECTS OF THE CONVENTION

The Hague Convention is designed to promote a speedy, summary return of children who have been wrongfully removed from, or retained outside, their countries of habitual residence. The welfare of abducted children is at the root of this Convention in that it seeks to ensure that the effects of an abduction are minimised, in particular by returning children as quickly as possible to the country from which they have been abducted and so allowing decisions on any underlying custody issues to be taken by the courts of the child's country of habitual residence. As well as minimising the effect of abductions that have taken place, the Convention is designed to deter future abductions, by making it clear that abducted children will be returned. It is not, however, designed to enforce or provide a decision on custody between parents or other carers. Despite its relatively Draconian aspect, the Convention seeks to encourage a voluntary resolution of individual cases where possible.

Applications are usually made on behalf of the parent or other person seeking a return by one contracting State ('the requesting State') to another ('the requested State'), and are usually channeled through the central authorities established in each Hague Convention country for this purpose. The description of the Convention which follows is introductory only, and is not intended as a manual for use in litigation, In particular, it should be noted that whilst the general principles are universal, inevitably there are differences of approach and interpretation as between Hague Convention contracting States, and some articles have not been adopted in some countries. (For full text, see later in Part 1.)

WRONGFUL REMOVAL OR RETENTION OF A CHILD

The key to the Hague Convention is the concept of wrongful removal from, or wrongful retention outside, the requesting State set out in Articles 3 and 12.

The elements required for a wrongful removal or retention are these. First, a child must have been habitually resident in the requesting State immediately before the removal or retention. Second, the removal or retention must have been an act committed in breach of some aspects of the rights of custody attributed to the applicant person, according to the laws of the requesting State. A right to determine the place (and therefore the country) of residence of the child, or to have a say in a decision on any change of place of residence, is an obvious example of a right breached by a non-consensual, or clandestine, removal or retention. Third, those rights of custody must have been actually exercised by the applicant parent, or would have been exercised but for the removal or retention. If these elements are established, and proceedings for a return are commenced in the requested State within 12 months of the removal or retention, the court of that State must order a return forthwith.

DEFENCES TO AN APPLICATION

There are limited defences, which are set out in Article 13, and which, if made out, give the court a discretion not to order a return. Article 13(a) provides a defence where the applicant parent has consented to the removal or the retention, or has subsequently acquiesced to it. If the removal or retention can be demonstrated to have been consensual, it may also be shown not to have been wrongful at all, and the application will fail without recourse to the discretion. Article 13(b) is child-centred, and provides a defence where to return a child would expose the child to a grave risk of physical or psychological harm, or place him or her in an intolerable situation. In most Convention countries, these words are taken literally, and there is a very high threshold – compared to that which would move the court on a welfare basis in ordinary private law children's cases – to an Article 13(b) defence. Article 13 also provides a limited voice for the child; there is a defence if the child objects to being returned, and has reached an age or degree of maturity at which it is appropriate to take account of his or her views. Countries vary in their approach to children's objections, in particular as to the interpretation of the threshold criteria of age and degree of maturity, and to the weight to be given to children's expressed views. Some countries routinely provide for the separate representation of children in Convention cases, whilst in other countries this is wholly exceptional. Additionally, Article 12 provides that if proceedings are commenced after 12 months from the date of removal or retention, there is a discretion not to return a child if it is demonstrated that the child is settled in his or her new environment. Most countries make some use of domestic welfare services, often court appointed, where information is required. Provision is made for international co-operation by the central authorities for the supply of reports and information where necessary. Sometimes this is achieved through International Social Services, sometimes through the instruction of domestic welfare services by the central authority in the requesting State.

DECLARATIONS AS TO WRONGFUL REMOVAL OR RETENTION

As will be seen, the need to demonstrate propositions of law from the requesting State in proceedings in the requested State arises from Article 3, especially as to rights of custody and their breach. Article 15 provides that a declaration as to whether a removal or retention was wrongful in the domestic law of the requesting State can be made by the courts of that country, so that problems of interpreting or proving foreign law in the courts of the requested State are avoided as far as is possible. Article 15 declarations are persuasive but not binding upon the courts of the requested State. Usually, they carry very considerable weight, but their usefulness in the context of the Convention often depends on the speed with which they can be procured, and the level of court which makes the declaration.

MEANING OF CONVENTION TERMS

Definition of terms, where not provided internally, is assisted by the 'Explanatory Report' which accompanies the Convention, and of course by case-law in the individual contracting States. Habitual residence is the key to the Convention, and is a question of fact. The habitual residence of childen is usually discerned from their physical whereabouts, and the settled intention as to residence of the parent or parents who are looking after them. A wrongful removal or retention cannot of itself change a child's habitual residence. The Convention has sought to avoid defining habitual residence in a restricted way, but the courts of many contracting States have spent time considering how, and over what period, habitual residence can be gained and lost. Rights of custody is a broad concept under the Convention. It is sometimes said to be broader than a strict interpretation of the domestic law of a contracting State might imply, and certainly includes a right to determine a child's place of residence. The rights given to unmarried fathers vary widely across Convention countries, as do the means by which such fathers become enfranchised where this is not automatic. This can lead to uncertainty in some Convention cases in particular where, in some countries, in some cases, inchoate rights have been discerned, which are deemed to be sufficient for Convention purposes, there are no substantive rights of custody in the domestic laws of the requesting State. Separate consideration is given to rights of access under the Convention, and a mere right of access may not be a right of custody. Whilst Article 21 gives scope for applications to secure the effective excercise of rights of access, there is not, in the view of a substantial number of contracting States, an express power to make orders under the Convention itself.

FUNDING OF LEGAL SERVICES

A substantial number of contracting States provide free legal services for the conduct of incoming applications under Article 26. Sometimes this is done by the provision of free legal aid to the applicant parent to allow the instruction of lawyers in private practice, via the central authority, but on what is, in effect, a lawyer and own client basis for the entirety of the Convention litigation. In some other Convention countries, free legal services are provided, but only by the State itself pursuing the application, for example, through the use of a public prosecutor or State attorney. In these cases, there is often less opportunity for direct access by the applicant parent to the lawyer who is running the case. In other countries, the practical and financial assistance for applicant parents is very limited. Abducting parents, seeking to defend Convention applications, may be entitled to legal aid in some countries, but in others they will have to be self-funding, or have to seek pro bono assistance if they wish to be represented.

EXPEDITION OF PROCEEDINGS

By the terms of the Convention, expedition of abduction cases is expressly required. In some countries, special arrangements are made for cases to come speedily before specialist judges at a central court, on short notice. In other countries, the existing, decentralised, court structure for ordinary family cases is employed. Convention cases are normally given priority over domestic litigation in respect of the same children in the requested State (characteristically started by the abducting parent after arrival).

THE EUROPEAN CONVENTION

OBJECTIVES OF THE CONVENTION

The European Convention is an order-based Convention, designed to provide mutual enforceability of decisions on custody and access between contracting States. Unlike the Hague Convention, it therefore has the capacity not simply to return the children who have been abducted internationally, but to return them to their custodial parents, and also to provide specific enforcement internationally of rights of access. As with the description of the Hague Convention above, this is not intended to be a comprehensive survey. (For full text, see pp 29 *et seq.*)

ENFORCEABILITY OF CUSTODY AND ACCESS ORDERS

This Convention also makes use of central authorities as the usual vehicle for the transmission of requests. The root of the Convention is Article 7 which simply provides that a decision relating to custody which is enforceable in the initiating country ('the State of origin') shall be enforceable in every other contracting State. Article 11 extends this principle to decisions on access but allows the court of the receiving country ('the State addressed') some latitude in fixing the conditions for enforcement. This latitude will not allow for a reconsideration of the substance of the original decision.

In normal circumstances, decisions for enforcement will have been made in regular proceedings in the State of origin, inter partes, before the child was removed internationally. However, there are limited provisions which are of particular relevance where the abducting parent has concealed his or her whereabouts, and which can render ex parte or retrospective orders eligible for enforcement. These are contained in Articles 9 (styled as defences) and 12, which also makes a declaratory provision. This is in plain contrast to the Hague Convention, where without exception the Article 3 criteria must be present at the date of removal or retention.

DEFENCES TO APPLICATIONS

The defences are found in Articles 9 and 10 and, as with the Hague Convention, provide a discretion not to recognise and enforce if they are made out. They are relatively intricate in their construction, and what follows is only a rough guide. In essence, they make enforcement optional where (subject to the principle set out above) the decision was not made on notice, was incompatible with a decision enforceable in the State addressed before the removal from the state of origin, or where the child was habitually resident in the State addressed. There are caveats to all these preparations. There are also defences more directly related to the welfare interests of the child, providing a discretion not to enforce if the effects of the original decision are 'manifestly incompatible with the fundamental principles of the law relating to the family and the children' in the State addressed, and where a change of circumstances has rendered the original decision 'manifestly no longer in accordance with the welfare of the child'. Like the Hague Convention defences under Article 13(b), there is usually a high threshold to be met.

In this order-based Convention, any temptation to review the substance of the foreign decisions is specifically excluded by Article 9(3) but, in addition to the defences above, an application for recognition and enforcement may be adjourned if the original decision is under appeal or review, or if proceedings which pre-date those in the State of origin are pending in the State addressed.

FUTURE DEVELOPMENTS IN RELATION TO CHILD ABDUCTION

THE HAGUE CONVENTION

The Hague Convention has proved popular and effective. The number of contracting States is currently 44, and is still growing. Early members were highly-developed countries with sophisticated systems of child law, and had little difficulty operating in comity with each other. Inevitably, where countries with disparate levels of economic and political development, and contrasting systems of law, sign the same Convention, some diversity of approach results, and the instinctive pull towards comity may be reduced. It is, however, a fundamental tenet of the Convention that each contracting State must trust the others to deal fairly with cases of returning children, as well as with applications for returns. Few real problems have emerged to date, in part, perhaps, because some signatories have generated very little, or no, child abduction traffic. Membership is by application, followed by ratification with other individual contracting States. Two factors may limit the further development of the membership list:

(1) the ability to set up the necessary administrative structure, which can be a considerable burden for some countries; and

(2) the need to demonstrate a system of law in children's cases which is based firmly on welfare principles so that the return of children is addressed in a manner which is internationally acceptable. Where aspects of a nation's own system of law is incompatible with the Convention which results, for example in custody decisions between parents being based in whole or in part on religious precepts, this may prove an obstruction to membership of the Convention.

FUTURE SIGNATORIES TO THE HAGUE CONVENTION

In future, existing contracting States may find there is a difficult balance to draw. By welcoming new countries into the Convention in the hope that returns which are currently difficult or impossible will be facilitated, should greatly assist existing contracting States' own nationals when children are abducted to those countries. However, if the Convention is to work properly, existing States will also have to return children (including their own nationals) to those new countries without questioning the fairness of their domestic systems of law.

BILATERAL TREATIES

Where a country does not become a Convention signatory, perhaps because its system of law or its political stance make it incompatible, there is likely to be a development of bilateral treaties. Some of these may provide for the return of children, perhaps between individual countries which share mutually compatible systems of law. However, bilateral Conventions which have more modest aims – for example, to secure a right of access to abducted children, or information about their whereabouts, or to provide an arbitration scheme whereby at least some of the difficulties arising from an abduction can be resolved – may be the way to assist children and their parents where fully comity is impossible.

THE EUROPEAN CONVENTION

The European Convention has as its parties a geographically, economically, and politically cohesive group of countries, with land borders, and free – in some cases, deliberately unrestricted – movement of their populations across them. Each member State also has a sophisticated and well-developed system of child law based firmly on welfare. The scope for enlargement of membership is necessarily limited. It is more likely that use of the Convention will increase. It is also plain that many European Community countries are striving for a uniformity of approach to, and applicability of, laws and decisions. This is likely to result in further conventions and agreements, extending the mutual enforceability of decisions, and effectively preventing the establishment of competing jurisdictions in children's cases, perhaps eventually resulting in a uniform code.

OTHER CONVENTIONS

International Conventions which are not specifically directed towards child abduction, including the United Nations Convention on the Rights of Children and the European Convention on Human Rights, are likely also to have an increasing impact as they enter the domestic laws of contracting States. Equally, extradition treaties, usually bilateral, are, and will increasingly be, used to seek the return of abducting parents, although the impact of criminal prosecutions or threats of prosecution can be unproductive when the position of abducted children is considered in the context of Convention applications.

The European Agreement on the Transmission of Legal Aid Applications 1977

This treaty, sometimes referred to as the Strasbourg Agreement, permits the transmission of applications for civil legal aid between signatory states. Signatory countries are:

Austria	Norway
Belgium	Portugal
Denmark	Republic of Ireland
France	Sweden
Greece	Turkey
Italy	United Kingdom
Luxembourg	

Each signatory has a designated Transmitting and Receiving Authority. This is usually the national Legal Aid Office or equivalent. Application is made by completing the standard legal aid application and means test form of the country transmitting the request, plus the requisite supporting documentation. Generally, this work will be carried out by the applicant's lawyer. Applications are accepted in the language of the transmitting jurisdiction. France and Austria require all documentation to be accompanied by translations. However, for expediency, it is advised to translate forms and documentation into the language of the receiving jurisdiction.

The receiving authority will base its assessment on the criteria for legal aid provision operating within its own jurisdiction. Consequently, an apparently adequate application made in one country may not be successful in another country. In other words, this procedure cannot guarantee that legal aid will be forthcoming. The receiving authority will notify the transmitting authority of the outcome of an assessment and also communicate reasons for any delay in this process if requested.

It should be noted that a successful application may also secure the services of a nominated 'legal aid' lawyer and, occasionally, such an appointment may not lead the applicant to a lawyer with specific experience in Convention or child abduction cases.

Some countries are willing to fund the preparation of an application and translation prior to transfer. For further guidance contact the Transmitting and Receiving Authority (Legal Aid Office) within your jurisdiction.

Islamic family law

INTRODUCTION

Family lawyers and other professionals practising in the field of child abduction are inevitably confronted by systems of law which are alien to them. There follows a brief introduction to the tenets of Islamic family law with which practitioners increasingly need to concern themselves. Bearing in mind the diversity of practice in Islamic jurisdictions, it should be regarded as a general guide only.

The Muslim faith has a worldwide following of over 6 billion people, the majority of whom reside in countries where Islam is the state religion. The Muslim world stretches beyond the Gulf states to South East Asia and across the North of Africa in the west.

Islam places great emphasis on personal conduct and duty. The Quran sets out a code of general principles which regulate both the individual's spiritual relationship with God and their relationships with others. This is the foundation of Islamic law known as the Sharia (also Shari'ah or Shariat) meaning the 'path of the believer' or Divine law. Further guidance is provided by records of traditions, ie sayings, deeds or tacit assents attributed to the Prophet Mohammed referred to as the Sunna. As the religion grew over the centuries, legal scholarship developed subordinate sources of law. *Ijma* (meaning consensus) represents the interpretations of early Islamic jurists who formulated the classical law. *Qiyas* (or analogy) is a method of development whereby similar cases decided using the higher legal authorities are extended by analogy to new factual situations. In other words, Islamic jurisprudence operates via a strictly adhered to hierarchy of sources flowing from the Quran down to the *Qiyas*. However, the interpretation of the Sharia will depend on the practice of different schools of law.

Within the context of Islamic jurisprudence, the concept of family law is strictly not recognised, but it would be understood by judges and lawyers practicising in Islamic countries. Family laws are found within the rules of personal status which govern a person's status, rights and duties within society. Unlike Western (Christian) societies, there is not always a clear division between the religious and secular (although, Turkey is an exception to this rule). The Sharia continues to be an important source of legal principle and in the sphere of personal status matters, its authority is predominant. For those Muslim families and communities residing in non-Islamic countries, the rules of personal status remain a powerful moral force.

THE DEVELOPMENT OF ISLAM

The rapid geographical spread of Islam and its widespread endorsement by different peoples has led to a divergence of interpretation. Political and theological differences led to the development of several schools of legal thought. Many of these doctrines have not survived, but those that have form the basis of contemporary Islamic belief in various countries.

The two main juristic sects existing in the present day are the Sunni and the Shia. There also exists the small sect of the Ibadis which will be discussed briefly later. Sunni Islam is the religion in its orthodox or traditional form representing the mainstream of Islamic jurisprudence and theology. Approximately 90 per cent of Muslims are followers referred to as Sunni Muslims. Shia Islam, whose adherents are termed Shi'ite Muslims, emerged due to a constitutional and political rift over the leadership of the Islamic community which occurred in the years following the Prophet's death. Early Sunnis believed that membership of the Prophet's tribe and consensus of the community were sufficient qualification for leadership while the Shi'ites held that only Mohammed's descendants could be eligible, having a divine right to rule. Thus, a Shi'ite leader or Imam is seen as divinely inspired and is accepted as the supreme authority on earth in matters religious and secular. *Ijmas* and *Qiyas* have a smaller place in Shi'ite jurisprudence which also rejects pre-Islamic and customary legal concepts. Instead, the source that is used after the Quran and the Sunna is the sayings of the Imam, of which the first 12 are particularly authoritative. This is the central distinction between Sunni and Shia Islam.

The Ibadis are a splinter from a larger earlier group called the Kharijites (outsiders) who were opposed to the idea of qualification through descent from Mohammed or his tribe and instead selected their leaders by free election on the basis of ability and religious learning. Closer to Sunni thinking than modern Shia, Ibadis observe the Sunna, extending traditions to include those of their two earliest leaders. They accept *Ijma* and *Qiyas* and are tolerant of other forms of Islam. It is the official doctrine in Oman and is practised in small parts of East Africa and Zanzibar. However, due to its comparatively small following, it is not discussed further in this book.

Sunni and Shia Islam have continued to evolve and a number of sub-groups, or schools, have appeared within each faction. Today, many of these schools co-exist, frequently alongside other faiths, within the same jurisdiction. Many States, particularly where a Sunni following prevails, have formulated their laws along pluralist lines. Thus variations may not always follow topographic boundaries and slight differences regarding interpretation and practice exist between the countries mentioned in this book.

SUNNI

The four major Sunni schools of law are as follows:

THE HANAFIS

This is the largest and most pragmatic of all the Muslim schools of law with a large following in Turkey, Albania, Afghanistan, Pakistan, India, Bangladesh, parts of Iraq, Jordan, Eygpt, China and ex-Yugoslavia. Hanafi law was the official school of law of the Ottoman Empire. The Ottoman Civil Code of 1876 (the Mejelle) was the first attempt to codify Islamic law. The Mejelle, however, did not touch personal status law. This was not codified by the Ottomans until the Ottoman Law of Family Rights 1917. These reforms have had a significant impact on the legislative development of the States that had made up the Ottoman Empire (which would now be identified as the Middle East) in particular Syria, Iraq, Jordan, Lebanon as well as Pakistan and Kuwait.

THE MALIKIS

Followers reside in parts of Eastern Arabia, the Gulf States, the Sudan, North and West Africa. It is based upon the law school of Medina in Saudi Arabia and is in some ways, more conservative than Hanafi law. However, it allows a role for public policy which other schools do not.

THE SHAFIIS

This school has a large following with about half living in South East Asia, Indonesia, Thailand, Singapore, Malaysia and Sri Lanka. The remainder are located in parts of East Africa and Eygpt. The Shafiis support the theory of the four sources as it was promulgated by Shafii himself. They also admit some other lesser sources of law.

THE HANBALIS

This is the most conservative of the Sunni sects and is the school of law of the Kingdom of Saudi Arabia and Qatar. There are also followers in some other Gulf States.

SHIA

The three major Shia sects are as follows:

THE ITHNA-ASHARIS (THE TWELVERS)

This is the largest of the Shi'ite sects. The origins of their faith are the teachings of the first 12 Imams, the last of whom is believed to be alive and will return near the end of time. In the absence of the twelfth Imam, authority, which remains paramount, rests with the Shia divines. Ithna-Asharism is concentrated in Iran where it has been the official doctrine for several hundred years. Other followers live in Pakistan, Iraq, Lebanon, Syria, Pakistan and Afghanistan.

THE ZAIYDIS

Followers reside mainly in Yemen and the school is regarded as being the nearest of the Shi'ite sects to Sunni Islam. They do not require their leader to be of divine descent and since 1961 the Imam no longer commands an overriding authority on secular matters.

THE ISMAILIS

Ismaili practice is concentrated in parts of India and in countries which have received immigrants from India. Their religious leader is the Aga Khan, who is a direct descendant of the Prophet Mohammed, and hence a living Imam. The Ismailis, through the authority of the Aga Khan, follow certain 'constitutions' which are amended from time to time.

GENERAL PRINCIPLES

LEGITIMACY

Marriage creates an assumption of paternity which may also be established by acknowledgement or evidence. Legitimacy defines the legal relationship between parent and child bestowing rights and duties of guardianship, custody and maintenance. Generally, a child's legitimacy will depend on the pre-natal marriage of his parents, a child born within six months of marriage will be illegitimate. Marriage between a Muslim woman and a non-Muslim man is not permitted so that a prospective husband must convert to Islam prior to entering a valid Muslim marriage. Marriage in any other form will be void and any resulting offspring will be illegitimate. Depending on their affiliation, some Muslim men are permitted to marry Kitabi women who are considered 'People of the Book', ie Jews and Christians, by the Sunnis. The Shi'ites include Magi women (worshippers of fire or Zoroastrians) in this category. This said, the Zaiydis forbid this practice. Legitimacy also confers the father's religion on the child, thus bringing decisions affecting the child under the authority of the Sharia.

ADOPTION

Adoption, in the Western sense, which places the adoptee on the same legal footing as a legitimate natural child, is not a concept recognised by Islamic law, although Tunisia and Turkey have exceptions in their domestic law. Consequently, in the unlikely event of dispute involving a child adopted in a non-Islamic jurisdiction, a question of conflict of laws may arise and specialist advice should be sought. However, this does not preclude Muslim families from taking responsibility for the long-term care of children who are not related to them or for children from their wider family circle and this is, in fact, common practice.

GUARDIANSHIP

Parental rights and responsibilities with reference to a child's upbringing are determined by the rules of guardianship. The performance of those rights and responsibilities is not automatically shared between parents. Under the Sharia, guardianship is divided into three areas, one of which is the custody of an infant. The other two are guardianship of education and guardianship of property, these are the responsibility of the father or male relatives. Different aspects of guardianship may run consecutively depending on the child's gender, age and needs. Any person exercising this authority is obliged to do so giving the child's interests paramount consideration.

CUSTODY DURING INFANCY OR CHILDHOOD

Custody or *hadana* (meaning raising) is the daily care of the infant or child during its early years. This is the only part of guardianship where the mother is acknowledged as having the superior claim. This principle has unanimous agreement throughout the Muslim world. A mother's right is terminable if her inability or ineligibility to undertake *hadana* is shown. If the mother is disqualified or unavailable to perform *hadana*, there is a hierarchy of appropriate relatives who can be appointed custodian in her place. The claim of an alternative custodian may be opposed. In general terms, preference is given to female maternal relatives, after whom the right will pass to female paternal relatives before passing to male relatives. The majority of Islamic countries have codified their chosen order of preference within personal status legislation. The right of *hadana* cannot prevent or overule a father or male relative from exercising his guardianship rights and, where parents are separated, it is accepted that the father continues to supervise the child's upbringing and pay for the child's maintenance.

CONDITIONS OF CUSTODY

Before any party, parent or not, can exercise the custody of an infant, specific conditions must be met:

(1) 'majority, sanity and freedom', ie not a slave; and
(2) the ability to rear the child, safeguard the child's interests and provide physical and moral protection, ie the custodian should not be too elderly or disabled or incapable of caring for the child. The custodian should not suffer a disease, be morally corrupt or working, although, if both parents work, adequate daytime child care arrangements are acceptable in some countries.

It is important to remember that moral standards and social norms are culturally subjective and that what constitutes acceptable behaviour in one country may not be viewed in the same way in another Islamic state. Fathers are obliged to pay for the child's care but there is no obligation to maintain the carer. Mothers without any other means of financial support may be required to work, thus rendering them vulnerable to disqualification. Where the mother, or any other female, is the sole custodian, extra requirements must be satisfied. These are:

MARRIAGE RESTRICTIONS

The custodian must not be married to a stranger. A stranger is a non-relative. The custodian must also not be married to a relative who is not prohibited from marrying the child. How strictly this rule is applied is usually clarified via legislation. Subsequent marriage will generally forfeit the right of custodianship for the duration of the marriage save where the Maliki tradition prevails which disqualifies custodianship permanently. If a subsequent marriage takes place, the right will pass to the next relative in the hadana hierarchy.

RELATIONSHIP

The custodian herself must be a non-prohibited relative, ie cannot marry the child.

RESIDENCE

The custodian and child must reside together in a home where the child is welcome.

RELIGION

The Ithna-Asharis and Shafiis believe that a non-Muslim woman is not eligible to rear a Muslim child, although it is acceptable where the mother is a Kitabi, ie a Christian or a Jew. All schools of Islamic tradition find grounds for disqualification if the custodian has rejected Islam. The primary concern is not so much the custodian's religion but her commitment to ensuring the child is brought up as a Muslim and not to influence the child otherwise. Some countries limit custodianship to a non-Muslim until the child reaches his fifth year.

Male custodianship of the infant is possible. A man with sole custodial authority must also be a prohibited relative, ie cannot marry a female child. The Shi'ite schools require any male custodian to follow the same religion as the child while other sects require the male custodian who is related to the father to be of the same religion as the child.

DURATION OF CUSTODY OF INFANT

The child has a right to be looked after from birth which is universal in Islamic tradition. The point of termination of that custody is determined by the child's gender, school of Islam, or the Civil Code of the State. Traditional rules are as follows:

THE HANAFIS

The dominant rule for boys is that the right to be looked after in infancy continues until the age of seven when a boy is considered to have reached a degree of independence, ie he is able to dress and feed himself without supervision.

For girls infancy ends at puberty which is generally considered to be at nine years of age.

THE MALIKIS

For boys, custody runs until puberty; for girls until their marriage. This means that, where there are two living parents, a child can stay with his mother overnight, but his education will be supervised by the father during the day.

THE SHAFIIS

There is no distinction based on gender. *Hadana* will continue until the child can make his own choice. As to when a child has reached this stage is a matter for the parents to decide together. If a boy chooses to remain with his mother, he can stay with her overnight but he must spend his days with his father. A girl choosing her mother will remain with her at all times.

THE HANBALIS

Custody will terminate when a child reaches seven years of age. The child is then permitted to choose with which parent he wishes to reside.

THE ITHNA-ASHARIS

Infancy ceases in the case of boys at the age of two years when they are deemed weaned and for girls at the age of seven years, although removal of the child from the mother should not take place if it is detrimental to the child. Conversely, the father has the right to remove the child from the mother earlier if her care is considered to be harmful.

RESIDENCE

On divorce, it is permitted for a mother with custody to leave the matrimonial home, but she must reside in a place sufficiently near to the father to allow him to visit the child and return home within a day. Relocation to the mother's home town or the district or town she was married in are exceptions to this. Any other destination will require the father's consent.

ACCESS

Custodians are obliged to give a natural parent access to a child. If necessary, either party can refuse access visits in their own home, but they must ensure that access takes place elsewhere. There is no rule on the frequency of access, but it is generally held to be a minimum of once a week. Access rights for grandparents and the wider family may also be recognised, but these will not be so frequent.

TRAVEL RIGHTS

A custodial mother can travel within a State without permission. However, she will not be permitted to leave the jurisdiction without the father's permission. Custodians who are not the mother of the child cannot travel anywhere without paternal consent. The Hanafis stipulate that a father with the right of access cannot travel with the child without the mother's consent. If the child's custodian is neither parent, commonly a female relative, the father is free to travel with the child. The remaining Sunni schools allow a father to travel with a child regardless of who holds *hadana*. The Ithna-Asharis permit a non-custodial father to travel with the child if the mother has lost *hadana*.

Organisations relevant to international child abduction cases

INTERPOL

THE FUNCTION OF INTERPOL

The International Criminal Police Organisation, or INTERPOL as it is most commonly known, is an intergovernmental organisation designed to facilitate police co-operation on an international basis. Interpol's primary function is the exchange of information, intelligence and evidence in criminal matters between member countries. Assistance will be provided in the investigation of 'ordinary law crime', but the Constitution forbids any involvement in matters of a political, racial, military or religious nature.

The world headquarters of Interpol is located in Lyon, France, and there are currently 178 full member countries plus 12 sub-bureaux throughout the world. Each member country has one Interpol National Central Bureau (NCB) which is normally located within a member State's capital city. NCBs are normally staffed by experienced police detectives from that country together with a number of civil support staff and work in accordance with that country's domestic laws and legal system. Interpol operates on a police to police basis. It does not ordinarily communicate directly with members of the general public. The public are advised to contact their local police for assistance.

Interpol bureaux around the world are organised in many different ways. For example, in London, the NCB is divided into sections which relate to specific types of crime. One section deals with all offences against the person covering murder, sexual offences, illegal immigration, paedophile offences, aviation offences, environmental crime, kidnap and child abduction.

In order to assist with the investigation of international child abduction cases, each Interpol member country will operate under the terms of its relevant child abduction legislation. In the UK, this is the Child Abduction Act 1984 which makes a criminal offence of unlawfully removing a child, under 16 years, from the UK. In some countries, there is no equivalent criminal offence which makes Interpol's job in London more difficult.

At Interpol London an enquiry relating to child abduction is generally commenced only when a formal request from a UK police service or a foreign Interpol bureau has been received. Experience indicates that by the time a request for assistance has been received from a UK police service, the abduction has taken place and the abducted child has already been removed from the UK jurisdiction. The primary task, therefore, is to initiate dialogue with the relevant foreign Interpol bureau with a view to locating the abducted child. If appropriate, Interpol London can also arrange to confirm that the child is safe and well which is often all that the foreign police service has the power to do. Their power to act will depend upon their own national legislation and specific details of a particular case.

To a large extent, Interpol London will rely upon the requesting police service to supply full and good quality information relating to the circumstances of the abduction and the likely location of the abducted child abroad. This will enhance the chances of the child being located quickly. The ability of a country to assist varies. There can be geographic, cultural, legal and procedural problems to overcome. In some countries, this type of offence simply may not be a priority.

THE ROLE OF INTERPOL IN THE CIVIL PROCESS

If the abducted child is located within the jurisdiction of a country which is a signatory to either the Hague or European Conventions on Child Abduction then Interpol can liaise with the UK Central Authority and, where appropriate, with the lawyer acting for the aggrieved parent/carer. The UK Central Authority will then arrange to make an application to the Central Authority of the country in which the child is located for the child's repatriation.

If the abducted child is located within a country which is not a signatory to either Convention then the repatriation of the child can be difficult, lengthy and expensive. Generally, the only method to repatriate from a non-Convention country is for the aggrieved parent/carer to commence civil proceedings in that country and in accordance with their laws. Interpol cannot assist in this process.

THE ROLE OF INTERPOL IN THE CRIMINAL PROCESS

In every case of child abduction in the UK, there is at least one offender who has committed the criminal offence of unlawful abduction. This is often one of the child's natural parents.

Over and above locating the abducted child and ensuring that it is safe and well, Interpol also takes responsibility for locating those persons who have committed the criminal offence. Once located, Interpol channels can be used to request the arrest and extradition of these offenders if this course of action is authorised by the competent judicial authority of the requesting country.

In England and Wales, the competent authority responsible for the prosecution of this type of criminal offence is the Crown Prosecution Service. For Scotland and Northern Ireland, it is the Crown Office and the Northern Ireland Office respectively. Interpol London, will only request the provisional arrest and extradition of any offender located abroad once this course of action has been authorised by one of these authorities.

It is appropriate to note that, even if an offender is located abroad, the competent authority will not automatically seek his arrest and extradition. The existence and terms of an Extradition Treaty with the finding country and the sufficiency of evidence are factors which must be taken into account when considering making an application for extradition.

In order to obtain the co-operation of the police services of a foreign country, contact must be made with the National Central Bureau of Interpol in the country in which the offence took place. Legal practitioners should do this through the police agency investigating the matter. All relevant information should be incorporated into a report including as much detail as possible about the likely location of the child and abductor. The National Central Bureau of Interpol will initiate enquiries abroad which are relevant to the circumstances of the particular case.

The successful conclusion of this type of offence will depend largely on the provision in the first instance of accurate information concerning the itinerary or destination of the persons concerned. This will allow enquiries to be forwarded to the most appropriate Interpol bureau and, subsequently, to the most appropriate local police service.

In the absence of specific information about destination, each Interpol bureau has the ability to send broadcast messages to all member countries or groups of member countries. This form of 'diffusion' message will result in the most appropriate supporting action being taken by the recipient country. Every diffusion will supply full personal details of the abducted child and any offender together with full circumstances of the abduction and details of any court orders currently in force. The diffusion will request each member State to conduct enquiries within their own jurisdiction with a view to locating the abducted child.

In certain cases, particularly those which can only be resolved in the longer term, each Interpol National Central Bureau can arrange for the publication of an Interpol Notice. These will be distributed throughout the member countries. These Notices contain all available information relating to personal details of the subject, a full summary of the facts of the case, the reason for the issue of the notice together with identification material such as photographs, fingerprints and, where appropriate, dental records, if available.

A Notice can be prepared in relation to:

(1) the abducted child; and/or
(2) the offender.

The Notices are prepared at the Interpol Headquarters in Lyon, France in English, French, Spanish and Arabic.

In general terms, this summary describes the role of Interpol in international child abduction enquiries. It should be stressed, however, that every country has its own sovereign laws, legal system, police procedures and protocol. These factors dictate the ability of the police services of a foreign country to assist. It is essential that legal practitioners and police investigators remain realistic in their expectations of what can be achieved.

INTERNATIONAL SOCIAL SERVICES

The International Social Services (ISS) is an independent voluntary charity operating autonomously from an internationally funded body. Described as an agency's agency, it can provide a point of contact between welfare services in different countries. The organisation's main concern is the provision of intercountry social work liaison services focussing on individual and family problems across international borders.

Its role with reference to abduction is ambiguous depending on the individual policy of the national bureau and whether the country involved is a signatory to the Hague Convention. The ISS will assist only if there is a child welfare issue in question which cannot be resolved through other means and it should be noted that the standard of welfare provision is determined by policy and funding. Therefore, the ISS will appear to be more effective in some countries than others.

The ISS will assist with 'safe and well' checks, provide international welfare reports and/or reports in support of an application for consent to leave or as part of a custody hearing. Any report will concentrate on the social assessment of the people involved with the care of the child and will not place emphasis on environmental factors. The actual reporting may be undertaken by local social workers or court welfare officers or their equivalent.

Depending on the country involved the ISS may assist with mediation, obtaining official records and provide further contacts with welfare services and other non-governmental organisations.

The ISS cannot fund litigation. Occasionally the ISS will provide financial assistance on the settlement of a custody dispute if a parent's lack of income could adversely affect a child's welfare, for example prevent the child from travelling home.

INTERNATIONAL RED CROSS

The International Red Cross does not have a direct interest in child abduction. Its presence within a State is usually due to a war or natural disaster. However, the organisation does provide an excellent tracing service. The ISS has close links with the International Red Cross and it is worth asking the ISS to liaise on a parent's behalf if other options have been exhausted.

The International Red Cross may prove particularly useful when dealing with countries where the UK has few links, for example, Iran and Iraq.

FOREIGN AND COMMONWEALTH OFFICE – CONSULAR SERVICES

THE FUNCTION OF THE FOREIGN AND COMMONWEALTH OFFICE CONSULAR SERVICES

The protection of all British nationals abroad is the primary responsibility of the Foreign and Commonwealth Office – Consular Services (FCO). Consequently, the plight of children taken overseas and that of the families they have left behind will immediately be treated as a matter of grave concern. Child abduction is now an established part of consular training. Staff are instructed how usefully to advise and support parents and the general issues surrounding the subject are discussed.

The Foreign and Commonwealth Office has staff in 188 countries consisting of 221 consulate posts whose officers generally undertake tours of three to four years, and a further 240 Honorary Consuls. In London, consular division desk officers, who are allocated regions or a country, act as a point of contact between parents and their colleagues overseas. Parents, relatives and their legal representatives should inform the FCO when travelling abroad to trace, visit, negotiate contact or return, or to initiate legal proceedings, particularly if the destination is a non-Convention country and/or they have no trusted contacts (see 'Travel Advice Unit' below).

It is crucial that parents understand that consular staff cannot automatically bring about a child's recovery and return. They have no authority to override the laws of another country and will be required to work with whatever resources are available to them. A high proportion of abductions involve children who are dual nationals. Thus, they are also nationals of the country to which they have been abducted. This prohibits the FCO from officially intervening and restricts the practical assistance that can be offered. Hence, the nature and level of assistance will vary from one country to another.

SERVICES AVAILABLE

The following services are available from the FCO:

- details of local lawyers who are able to correspond in English, and identifying family lawyers with child abduction expertise;
- co-operation in the notarising and transfer of court orders and other legal documents if legal proceedings ensue overseas;
- general advice on parental rights under the local and customary law;
- endeavouring to trace the child and establishing initial communication and continuing to act as a point of contact. This is particularly important where the child is unlikely to return;
- promoting amicable settlement by helping to arrange visits, providing a neutral meeting place and facilitating contact by telephone and letter;
- visiting the child to make a 'safe and well' check and/or liaising with local social service to obtain a welfare report;
- giving practical advice regarding accommodation and help with language difficulties;
- if the child is permitted to leave the country, issuing travel documents and ensuring the child is safe during its return.

SERVICES NOT AVAILABLE FROM FCO

the following services are *not* available from the FCO:

- the FCO cannot become involved in illegal attempts to return the child to the UK. The majority of countries would regard such action as abduction.
- it cannot pay legal expenses or the cost of repatriation.

TRAVEL ADVICE UNIT

This service provides regularly updated advice, in the form of Notices, to British travellers to help them avoid trouble. This information is largely orientated toward the tourist. However, their contents are practical, identifying regions experiencing political disruption, lawlessness, terrorism, etc, and situations where personal safety and health could be jeopardised.

Notices are distributed to the travel industry. Further dissemination is via the following:

Internet: http://www.fco.gov.uk/
BBC2 Ceefax: page 564 onwards
Travel Advice Unit: Tel 0171 238 4503/4504
Automated Telephone Service: 0374 500 900

REUNITE

reunite: the International Child Abduction Centre, formerly *reunite*: the National Council for Abducted Children is a UK-based charity which was established in May 1990. *reunite* provides a telephone advice line which offers advice and information to parents and families who have experienced parental child abduction or those who fear abduction. *reunite* also provides information to potential primary carer abductors wishing to return to the UK. Through the advice given, *reunite* is often in a position to prevent a potential abduction by making the parent aware of the international Conventions and the correct legal procedures that need to be followed before removing the child or children.

The *reunite* advice line is open daily Monday to Friday and the organisation provides out-of-hours emergency cover to ensure that no parent is left without immediate help.

reunite is recognised internationally and has assisted parents and other organisations all over the world. It works closely with other non-governmental organisations, worldwide. The charity works in partnership with the Parliamentary All Party Group on Child Abduction which was formed in 1990. This group has ensured that child abduction has stayed firmly on the political agenda and has seen the development of a child abduction prevention pack for both parents and police within England and Wales. A long term project of *reunite* is to provide Child Abduction Prevention Packs to parents in other countries and help raise public awareness of this growing global problem.

The vital ingredients of *reunite*'s success have been networking on an international scale, gathering information and the exchange of information. *reunite* produces a 'Lawyers Listing' of international/national lawyers who have expertise in the field of international child abduction. This listing is produced to assist parents in identifying the appropriate lawyer for their case, and is distributed through the *reunite* advice line and information packs and is updated annually. In support of the Lawyers Listing, *reunite* provides a National Legal Advisory Panel of experts who are willing to support other lawyers when dealing with difficult cases.

reunite also provides training to professionals working in the field of abduction, from training with voluntary and statutory organisations to providing speakers to attend national and international conferences. This area of work continues to grow and assists in raising the profile of the organisation.

For further information on the work of *reunite*, contact:

reunite International Child Abduction Centre
PO Box 4
London
England
WC1X 3DX
Advice Line: +44 (0) 171 404 8356
Admin Line: +44 (0) 171 404 8357
Fax: +44 (0)171 242 1512
Email: reunite©dircon.co.ukjki

The Hague Convention

Convention adopted by the Fourteenth Session and signed on 25 October 1980.

CONVENTION ON THE CIVIL ASPECTS OF INTERNATIONAL CHILD ABDUCTION

The States signatory to the present Convention,

Firmly convinced that the interests of children are of paramount importance in matters relating to their custody,

Desiring to protect children internationally from the harmful effects of their wrongful removal or retention and to establish procedures to ensure their prompt return to the State of their habitual residence, as well as to secure protection for rights of access,

Have resolved to conclude a Convention to this effect, and have agreed upon the following provisions –

CHAPTER I – SCOPE OF THE CONVENTION

ARTICLE I

The objects of the present Convention are:

(a) to secure the prompt return of children wrongfully removed to or retained in any Contracting State; and

(b) to ensure that rights of custody and of access under the law of one Contracting State are effectively respected in the other Contracting States.

ARTICLE 2

Contracting States shall take all appropriate measures to secure within their territories the implementation of the objects of the Convention. For this purpose they shall use the most expeditious procedures available.

ARTICLE 3

The removal or the retention of a child is to be considered wrongful where –

(a) it is in breach of rights of custody attributed to a person, an institution or any other body, either jointly or alone, under the law of the State in which the child was habitually resident immediately before the removal or retention; and

(b) at the time of removal or retention those rights were actually exercised, either jointly or alone, or would have been so exercised but for the removal or retention.

The rights of custody mentioned in sub-paragraph (a) above, may arise in particular by operation of law or by reason of a judicial or administrative decision, or by reason of an agreement having legal effect under the law of that State.

ARTICLE 4

The Convention shall apply to any child who was habitually resident in a Contracting State immediately before any breach of custody or access rights. The Convention shall cease to apply when the child attains the age of 16 years.

ARTICLE 5

For the purposes of this Convention –

(a) 'rights of custody' shall include rights relating to the care of the person of the child and, in particular, the right to determine the child's place of residence;

(b) 'rights of access' shall include the right to take a child for a limited period of time to a place other than the child's habitual residence.

CHAPTER II – CENTRAL AUTHORITIES

ARTICLE 6

A Contracting State shall designate a Central Authority to discharge the duties which are imposed by the Convention upon such authorities.

Federal States, States with more than one system of law or States having autonomous territorial organizations shall be free to appoint more than one Central Authority and to specify the territorial extent of their powers. Where a State has appointed more than one Central Authority, it shall designate the Central Authority to which applications may be addressed for transmission to the appropriate Central Authority within that State.

ARTICLE 7

Central Authorities shall co-operate with each other and promote co-operation amongst the competent authorities in their respective States to secure the prompt return of children and to achieve the other objects of this Convention.

In particular, either directly or through any intermediary, they shall take all appropriate measures –

(a) to discover the whereabouts of a child who has been wrongfully removed or retained;
(b) to prevent further harm to the child or prejudice to interested parties by taking or causing to be taken provisional measures:
(c) to secure the voluntary return of the child or to bring about an amicable resolution of the issues;
(d) to exchange, where desirable, information relating to the social background of the child;
(e) to provide information of a general character as to the law of their State in connection with the application of the Convention;
(f) to initiate or facilitate the institution of judicial or administrative proceedings with a view to obtaining the return of the child and, in a proper case, to make arrangements for organizing or securing the effective exercise of rights of access;
(g) where the circumstances so require, to provide or facilitate the provision of legal aid and advice, including the participation of legal counsel and advisers;
(h) to provide such administrative arrangements as may be necessary and appropriate to secure the safe return of the child;
(i) to keep each other informed with respect to the operation of this Convention and, as far as possible, to eliminate any obstacles to its application.

CHAPTER III – RETURN OF CHILDREN

ARTICLE 8

Any person, institution or other body claiming that a child has been removed or retained in breach of custody rights may apply either to the Central

Authority of the child's habitual residence or to the Central Authority of any other Contracting State for assistance in securing the return of the child.

The application shall contain –

(a) Information concerning the identity of the applicant, of the child and of the person alleged to have removed or retained the child;
(b) where available, the date of birth of the child;
(c) the grounds on which the applicant's claim for return of the child is based;
(d) all available information relating to the whereabouts of the child and the identity of the person with whom the child is presumed to be.

The application may be accompanied or supplemented by –

(e) an authenticated copy of any relevant decision or agreement;
(f) a certificate or an affidavit emanating from a Central Authority, or other competent authority of the State of the child's habitual residence, or from a qualified person, concerning the relevant law of that State;
(g) any other relevant document.

ARTICLE 9

If the Central Authority which receives an application referred to in Article 8 has reason to believe that the child is in another Contracting State, it shall directly and without delay transmit the application to the Central Authority of that Contracting State and inform the requesting Central Authority, or the applicant, as the case may be.

ARTICLE 10

The Central Authority of the State where the child is shall take or cause to be taken all appropriate measures in order to obtain the voluntary return of the child.

ARTICLE 11

The judicial or administrative authorities of Contracting States shall act expeditiously in proceedings for the return of children.

If the judicial or administrative authority concerned has not reached a decision within six weeks from the date of commencement of the proceedings, the applicant or the Central Authority of the requested State, on its own initiative or if asked by the Central Authority of the requesting State, shall have the right to request a statement of the reasons for the delay. If a reply is received by the Central Authority of the requested State, that Authority shall transmit the reply to the Central Authority of the requesting State, or to the applicant, as the case may be.

ARTICLE 12

Where a child has been wrongfully removed or retained in terms of Article 3 and, at the date of the commencement of the proceedings before the judicial or administrative authority of the Contracting State where the child is, a period of less than one year has elapsed from the date of the wrongful removal or retention, the authority concerned shall order the return of the child forthwith.

The judicial or administrative authority, even where the proceedings have been commenced after the expiration of the period of one year referred to in the preceding paragraph, shall also order the return of the child, unless it is demonstrated that the child is now settled in its new environment.

Where the judicial or administrative authority in the requested State has reason to believe that the child has been taken to another State, it may stay the proceedings or dismiss the application for the return of the child.

ARTICLE 13

Notwithstanding the provisions of the preceding Article, the judicial or administrative authority of the requested State is not bound to order the return of the child if the person, institution or other body which opposes its return establishes that –

(a) the person, institution or other body having the care of the person of the child was not actually exercising the custody rights at the time of removal or retention, or had consented to or subsequently acquiesced in the removal or retention; or
(b) there is a grave risk that his or her return would expose the child to physical or psychological harm or otherwise place the child in an intolerable situation.

The judicial or administrative authority may also refuse to order the return of the child if it finds that the child objects to being returned and has attained an age and degree of maturity at which it is appropriate to take account of its views.

In considering the circumstances referred to in this Article, the judicial and administrative authorities shall take into account the information relating to the social background of the child provided by the Central Authority or other competent authority of the child's habitual residence.

ARTICLE 14

In ascertaining whether there has been a wrongful removal or retention within the meaning of Article 3, the judicial or administrative authorities of the requested State may take notice directly of the law of, and of judicial or administrative decisions, formally recognized or not in the State of the habitual residence of the child, without recourse to the specific procedures for the proof of that law or for the recognition of foreign decisions which would otherwise be applicable.

ARTICLE 15

The judicial or administrative authorities of a Contracting State may, prior to the making of an order for the teturn of the child, request that the applicant obtain from the authorities of the State of the habitual residence of the child a decision or other determination that the removal or retention was wrongful within the meaning of Article 3 of the Convention, where such a decision or determination may be obtained in that State. The Central Authorities of the Contracting States shall so far as practicable assist applicants to obtain such a decision or determination.

ARTICLE 16

After receiving notice of a wrongful removal or retention of a child in the sense of Article 3, the judicial or administrative authorities of the Contracting State to which the child has been removed or in which it has been retained shall not decide on the merits of rights of custody until it has been determined that the child is not to be returned under this Convention or unless an application under this Convention is not lodged within a reasonable time following receipt of the notice.

ARTICLE 17

The sole fact that a decision relating to custody has been given in or is entitled to recognition in the requested State shall not be a ground for refusing to return a child under this Convention, but the judicial or administrative authorities of the requested State may take account of the reasons for that decision in applying this Convention.

ARTICLE 18

The provisions of this Chapter do not limit the power of a judicial or administrative authority to order the return of the child at any time.

ARTICLE 19

A decision under this Convention concerning the return of the child shall not be taken to be a determination on the merits of any custody issue.

ARTICLE 20

The return of the child under the provisions of Article 12 may be refused if this would not be permitted by the fundamental principles of the requested State relating to the protection of human rights and fundamental freedoms.

CHAPTER IV – RIGHTS OF ACCESS

ARTICLE 21

An application to make arrangements for organizing or securing the effective exercise of rights of access may be presented to the Central Authorities of the Contracting States in the sme way as an application for the return of a child.

The Central Authorities are bound by the obligations of co-operation which are set forth in Article 7 to promote the peaceful enjoyment of access rights and the fulfilment of any conditions to which the exercise of those rights may be subject. The Central Authorities shall take steps to remove, as far as possible, all obstacles to the exercise of such rights. The Central Authorities, either directly or through intermediaries, may initiate or assist in the institution of proceedings with a view to organizing or protecting these rights and securing respect for the conditions to which the exercise of these rights may be subject.

ARTICLE 22

No security, bond or deposit, however described, shall be required to guarantee the payment of costs and expenses in the judicial or administrative proceedings falling within the scope of this Convention.

ARTICLE 23

No legalization or similar formality may be required in the context of this Convention.

ARTICLE 24

Any application, communication or other document sent to the Central Authority of the requested State shall be in the original langauge, and shall be accompanied by a translation into the official language or one of the official languages of the requested State or, where that is not feasible, a translation into French or English.

However, a Contracting State may, by making a reservation in accordance with Article 42, object to the use of either French or English, but not both, in any application, communication or other document sent to its Central Authority.

ARTICLE 25

Nationals of the Contracting States and persons who are habitually resident within those States shall be entitled in matters concerned with the application of this Convention to legal aid and advice in any other Contracting State on the same conditions as if they themselves were nationals of and habitually resident in that State.

ARTICLE 26

Each Central Authority shall bear its own costs in applying this Convention.

Central Authorities and other public services of Contracting States shall not impose any charges in relation to applications submitted under this Convention. In particular, they may not require any payment from the applicant towards the costs and expenses of the proceedings or, where applicable, those arising from the participation of legal counsel or advisers. However, they may require the payment of the expenses incurred or to be incurred in implementing the return of the child.

However, a Contracting State may, by making a reservation in accordance with Article 42, declare that it shall not be bound to assume any costs referred to in the preceding paragraph resulting from the participation of legal counsel or advisers or from court proceedings, except insofar as those costs may be covered by its system of legal aid and advice.

Upon ordering the return of a child or issuing an order concerning rights of access under this Convention, the judicial or administrative authorities may, where appropriate, direct the person who removed or retained the child, or who prevented the exercise of rights of access, to pay necessary expenses incurred by or on behalf of the applicant, including travel expenses, any costs incurred or payments made for locating the child, the costs of legal representation of the applicant, and those of returning the child.

ARTICLE 27

When it is manifest that the requirements of this Convention are not fulfilled or that the applicant is otherwise not well founded, a Central Authority is not bound to accept the application. In that case, the Central Authority shall forthwith inform the applicant or the Central Authority through which the application was submitted, as the case may be, of its reasons.

ARTICLE 28

A Central Authority may require that the application be accompanied by a written authorization empowering it to act on behalf of the applicant, or to designate a representative so to act.

ARTICLE 29

This Convention shall not preclude any person, institution or body who claims that there has been a breach of custody or access rights within the meaning of Article 3 or 21 from applying directly to the judicial or administrative authorities of a Contracting State, whether or not under the provisions of this Convention.

ARTICLE 30

Any application submitted to the Central Authorities or directly to the judicial or administrative authorities of a Contracting State in accordance with the terms of this Convention, together with documents and any other information appended thereto or provided by a Central Authority, shall be admissible in the courts or administrative authorities of the Contracting States.

ARTICLE 31

In relation to a State which in matters of custody of children has two or more system of law applicable in different territorial units –

(a) any reference to habitual residence in that State shall be construed as referring to habitual residence in a territorial unit of that State;

(b) any reference to the law of the State of habitual residence shall be construed as referring to the law of the territorial unit in that State where the child habitually resides.

ARTICLE 32

In relation to a State which in matters of custody of children has two or more systems of law applicable to different categories of persons, any reference to the law of that State shall be construed as referring to the legal system specified by the law of that State.

ARTICLE 33

A State within which different territorial units have their own rules of law in respect of custody of children shall not be bound to apply this Convention where a State with a unified system of law would not be bound to do so.

ARTICLE 34

This Convention shall take priority in matters within its scope over the *Convention of 5 October 1961 concerning the powers of authorities and the law applicable in respect of the protection of minors*, as between Parties to both Conventions. Otherwise the present Convention shall not restrict the application of an international instrument in force between the State of origin and the State addressed or other law of the State addressed for the purposes of obtaining the return of a child who has been wrongfully removed or retained or of organizing access rights.

ARTICLE 35

This Convention shall apply as between Contracting States only to wrongful removals or retentions occurring after its entry into force in those States.

Where a declaration has been made under Article 39 or 40, the reference in the preceding paragraph to a Contracting State shall be taken to refer to the territorial unit or units in relation to which this Convention applies.

ARTICLE 36

Nothing in this Convention shall prevent two or more Contracting States, in order to limit the restrictions to which the return of the child may be subject, from agreeing among themselves to derogate from any provisions of this Convention which may imply such a restriction.

CHAPTER VI – FINAL CLAUSES

ARTICLE 37

The Convention shall be open for signature by the States which were Members of the Hague Conference on Private International Law at the time of its Fourteenth Session.

It shall be ratified, accepted or approved and the instruments of ratification, acceptance or approval shall be deposited with the Ministry of Foreign Affairs of the Kingdom of the Netherlands.

ARTICLE 38

Any other State may accede to the Convention.

The instrument of accession shall be deposited with the Ministry of Foreign Affairs of the Kingdom of the Netherlands.

The Convention shall enter into force for a State acceding to it on the first day of the third calendar month after the deposit of its instrument of accession.

The accession will have effect only as regards the relations between the acceding State and such Contracting States as will have declared their acceptance of the accession. Such a declaration will also have to be made by any Member State ratifying, accepting or approving the Convention after an accession. Such declaration shall be deposited at the Ministry of Foreign Affairs of the Kingdom of the Netherlands; this Ministry shall forward, through diplomatic channels, a certified copy to each of the Contracting States.

The Convention will enter into force as between the acceding State and the State that has declared its acceptance of the accession on the first day of the third calendar month after the deposit of the declaration of acceptance.

ARTICLE 39

Any State may, at the time of signature, ratification, acceptance, approval or accession, declare that the Convention shall extend to all the territories for the international relations of which it is responsible, or to one or more of them. Such a declaration shall take effect at the time the Convention enters into force for that State.

Such declaration, as well as any subsequent extension, shall be notified to the Ministry of Foreign Affairs of the Kingdom of the Netherlands.

ARTICLE 40

If a Contracting State has two or more territorial units in which different systems of law are applicable in relation to matters dealt with in this Convention, it may at the time of signature, ratification, acceptance, approval or accession declare that this Convention shall extend to all its territorial units or only to one or more of them and may modify this declaration by submitting another declaration at any time.

Any such declaration shall be notified to the Ministry of Foreign Affairs of the Kingdom of the Netherlands and shall state expressly the territorial units to which the Convention applies.

ARTICLE 41

Where a Contracting State has a system of government under which executive, judicial and legislative powers are distributed between central and other authorities within that State, its signature or ratification, acceptance or approval of, or accession to this Convention, or its making of any declaration in terms of Article 40 shall carry no implication as to the internal distribution of powers within that State.

ARTICLE 42

Any State may, not later than the time of ratification, acceptance, approval or accession, or at the time of making a declaration in terms of Article 39 or 40, made one or both of the reservations provided for in Article 24 and Article 26, third paragraph. No other reservation shall be permitted.

Any State may at any time withdraw a reservation it has made. The withdrawal shall be notified to the Ministry of Foreign Affairs of the Kingdom of the Netherlands.

The reservation shall cease to have effect on the first day of the third calendar month after the notification referred to in the preceding paragraph.

ARTICLE 43

The Convention shall enter into force on the first day of the third calendar month after the deposit of the third instrument of ratification, acceptance, approval or accession referred to in Articles 37 and 38.

Thereafter the Convention shall enter into force –

(1) for each State ratifying, accepting, approving or acceding to it subsequently, on the first day of the third calendar month after the deposit of its instrument of ratification, acceptance, approval or accession;

(2) for any territory or territorial unit to which the Convention has been extended in conformity with Article 39 or 40, on the first day of the third calendar month after the notification referred to in that Article.

ARTICLE 44

The Convention shall remain in force for five years from the date of its entry into force in accordance with the first paragraph of Article 43 even for States which subsequently have ratified, accepted, approved it or acceded to it.

If there has been no denunciation, it shall be renewed tacitly every five years.

Any denunciation shall be notified to the Ministry of Foreign Affairs of the Kingdom of the Netherlands at least six months before the expiry of the five year period. It may be limited to certain of the territories or territorial units to which the Convention applies.

The denunciation shall have effect only as regards the State which has notified it. The Convention shall remain in force for the other Contracting States.

ARTICLE 45

The Ministry of Foreign Affairs of the Kingdom of the Netherlands shall notify the States Members of the Conference, and the States which have acceded in accordance with Article 38, of the following –

(1) the signatures and ratifications, acceptances and approvals referred to in Article 37;

(2) the accessions referred to in Article 38;

(3) the date on which the Convention enters into force in accordance with Article 43;

(4) the extensions referred to in Article 39;

(5) the declarations referred to in Articles 38 and 40;

(6) the reservations referred to in Article 24 and Article 26, third paragraph, and the withdrawals referred to in Article 42;

(7) the denunciations referred to in Article 44.

In witness whereof the undersigned, being duly authorized thereto, have signed this Convention.

Done at The Hague, on the 25th day of October, 1980, in the English and French languages, both texts being equally authentic, in a single copy which shall be deposited in the archives of the Government of the Kingdom of the Netherlands, and of which a certified copy shall be sent, through diplomatic channels, to each of the States Members of the Hague Conference on Private International Law at the date of its Fourteenth Session.

The European Convention

Convention signed in Luxembourg on 20 May 1980.

The member States of the Council of Europe, signatory hereto,

Recognising that in the member States of the Council of Europe the welfare of the child is of overriding importance in reaching decisions concerning his custody;

Considering that the making of arrangements to ensure that decisions concerning the custody of a child can be more widely recognised and enforced will provide greater protection of the welfare of children;

Considering it desirable, with this end in view, to emphasise that the right of access of parents is a normal corollary to the right of custody;

Noting the increasing number of cases where children have been improperly removed across an international frontier and the difficulties of securing adequate solutions to the problems caused by such cases;

Desirous of making suitable provision to enable the custody of children which has been arbitrarily interrupted to be restored;

Convinced of the desirability of making arrangements for this purpose answering to different needs and different circumstances;

Desiring to establish legal co-operation between their authorities;

Have agreed as follows:

ARTICLE I

For the purposes of this Convention:

(a) *child* means a person of any nationality, so long as he is under 16 years of age and has not the right to decide on his own place of residence under the law of his habitual residence, the law of his nationality or the internal law of the State addressed;

(b) *authority* means a judicial or administrative authority;

(c) *decision relating to custody* means a decision of an authority in so far as it relates to the care of the person of the child, including the right to decide on the place of his residence, or to the right of access to him;

(d) *improper removal* means the removal of a child across an international frontier in breach of a decision relating to his custody which has been given in a Contracting State and which is enforceable in such a State; improper removal also includes:

(i) the failure to return a child across an international frontier at the end of a period of the exercise of the right of access to this child or at the end of any other temporary stay in a territory other than that where the custody is exercised;

(ii) a removal which is subsequently declared unlawful within the meaning of Article 12.

PART I

CENTRAL AUTHORITIES

ARTICLE 2

1. Each Contracting State shall appoint a central authority to carry out the functions provided for by this Convention.

2. Federal States and States with more than one legal system shall be free to appoint more than one central authority and shall determine the extent of their competence.

3. The Secretary General of the Council of Europe shall be notified of any appointment under this Article.

ARTICLE 3

1. The central authorities of the Contracting States shall co-operate with each other and promote co-operation between the competent authorities in their respective countries. They shall act with all necessary despatch.

2. With a view to facilitating the operation of this Convention, the central authorities of the Contracting States:

(a) shall secure the transmission of requests for information coming from competent authorities and relating to legal or factual matters concerning pending proceedings;

(b) shall provide each other on request with information about their law relating to the custody of children and any changes in that law;

(c) shall keep each other informed of any difficulties likely to arise in applying the Convention and, as far as possible, eliminate obstacles to its application.

ARTICLE 4

1. Any person who has obtained in a Contracting State a decision relating to the custody of a child and who wishes to have that decision recognised or

enforced in another Contracting State may submit an application for this purpose to the central authority in any Contracting State.

2. The application shall be accompanied by the documents mentioned in Article 13.

3. The central authority receiving the application, if it is not the central authority in the State addressed, shall send the documents directly and without delay to that central authority.

4. The central authority receiving the application may refuse to intervene where it is manifestly clear that the conditions laid down by this Convention are not satisfied.

5. The central authority receiving the application shall keep the applicant informed without delay of the progress of his application.

ARTICLE 5

1. The central authority in the State addressed shall take or cause to be taken without delay all steps which it considers to be appropriate, if necessary by instituting proceedings before its competent authorities, in order:

(a) to discover the whereabouts of the child;
(b) to avoid, in particular by any necessary provisional measures, prejudice to the interests of the child or of the applicant;
(c) to secure the recognition or enforcement of the decision;
(d) to secure the delivery of the child to the applicant where enforcement is granted;
(e) to inform the requesting authority of the measures taken and their results.

2. Where the central authority in the State addressed has reason to believe that the child is in the territory of another Contracting State it shall send the documents directly and without delay to the central authority of that State.

3. With the exception of the cost of repatriation, each Contracting State undertakes not to claim any payment from an applicant in respect of any measures taken under paragraph 1 of this Article by the central authority of that State on the applicant's behalf, including the costs of proceedings and, where applicable, the costs incurred by the assistance of a lawyer.

4. If recognition or enforcement is refused, and if the central authority of the State addressed considers that it should comply with a request by the applicant to bring in that State proceedings concerning the substance of the case, that authority shall use its best endeavours to secure the representation of the applicant in the proceedings under conditions no less favourable than

those available to a person who is resident in and a national of that State and for this purpose it may, in particular, institute proceedings before its competent authorities.

ARTICLE 6

1. Subject to any special agreements made between the central authorities concerned and to the provisions of paragraph 3 of this Article:

(a) communications to the central authority of the State addressed shall be made in the official language or in one of the official languages of that State or be accompanied by a translation into that language;
(b) the central authority of the State addressed shall nevertheless accept communications made in English or in French or accompanied by a translation into one of these languages.

2. Communications coming from the central authority of the State addressed, including the results of enquiries carried out, may be made in the official language or one of the official languages of that State or in English or French.

3. A Contracting State may exclude wholly or partly the provisions of paragraph 1(b) of this Article. When a Contracting State has made this reservation any other Contracting State may also apply the reservation in respect of that State.

PART II

RECOGNITION AND ENFORCEMENT OF DECISIONS AND RESTORATION OF CUSTODY OF CHILDREN

ARTICLE 7

A decision relating to custody given in a Contracting State shall be recognised and, where it is enforceable in the State of origin, made enforceable in every other Contracting State.

ARTICLE 8

1. In the case of an improper removal, the central authority of the State addressed shall cause steps to be taken forthwith to restore the custody of the child where:

(a) at the time of the institution of the proceedings in the State where the decision was given or at the time of the improper removal, if earlier, the child and his parents had as their sole nationality the nationality of that State and the child had his habitual residence in the territory of that State, and

(b) a request for the restoration was made to a central authority within a period of six months from the date of the improper removal.

2. If, in accordance with the law of the State addressed, the requirements of paragraph 1 of this Article cannot be complied with without recourse to a judicial authority, none of the grounds of refusal specified in this Convention shall apply to the judicial proceedings.

3. Where there is an agreement officially confirmed by a competent authority between the person having the custody of the child and another person to allow the other person a right of access, and the child, having been taken abroad, has not been restored at the end of the agreed period to the person having the custody, custody of the child shall be restored in accordance with paragraphs 1(b) and 2 of this Article. The same shall apply in the case of a decision of the competent authority granting such a right to a person who has not the custody of the child.

ARTICLE 9

1. In cases of improper removal, other than those dealt with in Article 8, in which an application has been made to a central authority within a period of six months from the date of the removal, recognition and enforcement may be refused only if:

(a) in the case of a decision given in the absence of the defendant or his legal representative, the defendant was not duly served with the document which instituted the proceedings or an equivalent document in sufficient time to enable him to arrange his defence; but such a failure to effect service cannot constitute a ground for refusing recognition or enforcement where service was not effected because the defendant had concealed his whereabouts from the person who instituted the proceedings in the State of origin;

(b) in the case of a decision given in the absence of the defendant or his legal representative, the competence of the authority giving the decision was not founded:

(i) on the habitual residence of the defendant, or

(ii) on the last common habitual residence of the child's parents, at least one parent being still habitually resident there, or

(iii) on the habitual residence of the child;

(c) the decision is incompatible with a decision relating to custody which became enforceable in the State addressed before the removal of the child, unless the child has had his habitual residence in the territory of the requesting State for one year before his removal.

2. Where no application has been made to a central authority, the provisions of paragraph 1 of this Article shall apply equally, if recognition and enforcement are requested within six months from the date of the improper removal.

3. In no circumstances may the foreign decision be reviewed as to its substance.

ARTICLE 10

1. In cases other than those covered by Articles 8 and 9, recognition and enforcement may be refused not only on the grounds provided for in Article 9 but also on any of the following grounds:

(a) if it is found that the effects of the decison are manifestly incompatible with the fundamental principles of the law relating to the family and children in the State addressed;
(b) if it is found that by reason of a change in the circumstances including the passage of time but not including a mere change in the residence of the child after an improper removal, the effects of the original decision are manifestly no longer in accordance with the welfare of the child;
(c) if at the time when the proceedings were instituted in the State of origin:
   (i) the child was a national of the State addressed or was habitually resident there and no such connection existed with the State of origin;
   (ii) the child was a national both of the State of origin and of the State addressed and was habitually resident in the State addressed;
(d) if the decision is incompatible with a decision given in the State addressed or enforceable in that State after being given in a third State, pursuant to proceedings begun before the submission of the request for recognition or enforcement, and if the refusal is in accordance with the welfare of the child.

2. In the same cases, proceedings for recognition or enforcement may be adjourned on any of the following grounds:

(a) if an ordinary form of review of the original decision has been commenced;

(b) if proceedings relating to the custody of the child, commenced before the proceedings in the State of origin were instituted, are pending in the State addressed;

(c) if another decision concerning the custody of the child is the subject of proceedings for enforcement or of any other proceedings concerning the recognition of the decision.

ARTICLE 11

1. Decisions on rights of access and provisions of decisions relating to custody which deal with the right of access shall be recognised and enforced subject to the same conditions as other decisions relating to custody.

2. However, the competent authority of the State addressed may fix the conditions for the implementation and exercise of the right of access taking into account, in particular, undertakings given by the parties on this matter.

3. Where no decision on the right of access has been taken or where recognition or enforcement of the decision relating to custody is refused, the central authority of the State addressed may apply to its competent authorities for a decision on the right of access, if the person claiming a right of access so requests.

ARTICLE 12

Where, at the time of the removal of a child across an international frontier, there is no enforceable decision given in a Contracting State relating to his custody, the provisions of this Convention shall apply to any subsequent decision, relating to the custody of that child and declaring the removal to be unlawful, given in a Contracting State at the request of any interested person.

PART III

PROCEDURE

ARTICLE 13

1. A request for recognition or enforcement in another Contracting State of a decision relating to custody shall be accompanied by:

(a) a document authorising the central authority of the State addressed to act on behalf of the applicant or to designate another representative for that purpose;

(b) a copy of the decision which satisfies the necessary conditions of authenticity;

(c) in the case of a decision given in the absence of the defendant or his legal representative, a document which establishes that the defendant was duly served with the document which instituted the proceedings or an equivalent document;

(d) if applicable, any document which establishes that, in accordance with the law of the State of origin, the decision is enforceable;

(e) if possible, a statement indicating the whereabouts or likely whereabouts of the child in the State addressed;

(f) proposals as to how the custody of the child should be restored.

2. The documents mentioned above shall, where necessary, be accompanied by a translation according to the provisions laid down in Article 6.

ARTICLE 14

Each Contracting State shall apply a simple and expeditious procedure for recognition and enforcement of decisions relating to the custody of a child. To that end it shall ensure that a request for enforcement may be lodged by simple application.

ARTICLE 15

1. Before reaching a decision under paragraph 1(b) of Article 10, the authority concerned in the State addressed:

(a) shall ascertain the child's views unless this is impracticable having regard in particular to his age and understanding; and

(b) may request that any appropriate enquiries be carried out.

2. The cost of enquiries in any Contracting State shall be met by the authorities of the State where they are carried out.

Requests for enquries and the results of enquiries may be sent to the authority concerned through the central authorities.

ARTICLE 16

For the purposes of this Convention, no legislation or any like formality may be required.

PART IV

RESERVATIONS

ARTICLE 17

1. A Contracting State may make a reservation that, in cases covered by Articles 8 and 9 or either of these Articles, recognition and enforcement of decisions relating to custody may be refused on such of the grounds provided under Article 10 as may be specified in the reservation.

2. Recognition and enforcement of decisions given in a Contracting State which has made the reservation provided for in paragraph 1 of this Article may be refused in any other Contracting State on any of the additional grounds referred to in that reservation.

ARTICLE 18

A Contracting State may make a reservation that it shall not be bound by the provisions of Article 12. The provisions of this Convention shall not apply to decisions referred to in Article 12 which have been given in a Contracting State which has made such a reservation.

PART V

OTHER INSTRUMENTS

ARTICLE 19

This Convention shall not exclude the possibility of relying on any other international instrument in force between the State of origin and the State addressed or on any other law of the State addressed not derived from an international agreement for the purpose of obtaining recognition or enforcement of a decision.

ARTICLE 20

1. This Convention shall not affect any obligations which a Contracting State may have towards a non-contracting State under an international instrument dealing with matters governed by this Convention.

2. When two or more Contracting States have enacted uniform laws in relation to custody of children or created a special system of recognition or enforcement of decisions in this field, or if they should do so in the future,

they shall be free to apply, between themselves, those laws or that system in place of this Convention or any part of it. In order to avail themselves of this provision the States shall notify their decision to the Secretary General of the Council of Europe. Any alteration or revocation of this decision must also be notified.

PART VI

FINAL CLAUSES

ARTICLE 21

This Convention shall be open for signature by the member States of the Council of Europe. It is subject to ratification, acceptance or approval. Instruments of ratification, acceptance or approval shall be deposited with the Secretary General of the Council of Europe.

ARTICLE 22

1. This Convention shall enter into force on the first day of the month following the expiration of a period of three months after the date on which three member States of the Council of Europe have expressed their consent to be bound by the Convention in accordance with the provisions of Article 21.

2. In respect of any member State which subsequently expresses its consent to be bound by it, the Convention shall enter into force on the first day of the month following the expiration of a period of three months after the date of the deposit of the instrument of ratification, acceptance or approval.

ARTICLE 23

1. After the entry into force of this Convention, the Committee of Ministers of the Council of Europe may invite any State not a member of the Council to accede to this Convention, by a decision taken by the majority provided for by Article 20(d) of the Statute and by the unanimous vote of the representatives of the Contracting States entitled to sit on the Committee.

2. In respect of any acceding State, the Convention shall enter into force on the first day of the month following the expiration of a period of three months after the date of deposit of the instrument of accession with the Secretary General of the Council of Europe.

ARTICLE 24

1. Any State may at the time of signature or when depositing its instrument of ratification, acceptance, approval or accession, specify the territory or territories to which this Convention shall apply.

2. Any State may at any later date, by a declaration addressed to the Secretary General of the Council of Europe, extend the application of this Convention to any other territory specified in the declaration. In respect of such territory, the Convention shall enter into force on the first day of the month following the expiration of a period of three months after the date of receipt by the Secretary General of such declaration.

3. Any declaration made under the two preceding paragraphs may, in respect of any territory specified in such declaration, be withdrawn by a notification addressed to the Secretary General. The withdrawal shall become effective on the first day of the month following the expiration of a period of six months after the date of receipt of such notification by the Secretary General.

ARTICLE 25

1. A State which has two or more territorial units in which different systems of law apply in matters of custody of children and of recognition and enforcement of decisions relating to custody may, at the time of signature or when depositing its instrument of ratification, acceptance, approval or accession, declare that this Convention shall apply to all its territorial units or to one or more of them.

2. Such a State may at any later date, by a declaration addressed to the Secretary General of the Council of Europe, extend the application of this Convention to any other territorial unit specified in the declaration. In respect of such territorial unit the Convention shall enter into force on the first day of the month following the expiration of a period of three months after the date of receipt by the Secretary General of such declaration.

3. Any declaration made under the two preceding paragraphs may, in respect of any territorial unit specified in such declaration, be withdrawn by notification addressed to the Secretary General. The withdrawal shall become effective on the first day of the month following the expiration of a period of six months after the date of receipt of such notification by the Secretary General.

ARTICLE 26

1. In relation to a State which has in matters of custody two or more systems of law of territorial application:

(a) reference to the law of a person's habitual residence or to the law of a person's nationality shall be construed as referring to the system of law determined by the rules in force in that State or, if there are no such rules, to the system of law with which the person concerned is most closely connected;

(b) reference to the State of origin or to the State addressed shall be construed as referring, as the case may be, to the territorial unit where the decision was given or to the territorial unit where recognition or enforcement of the decision or restoration of custody is requested.

2. Paragraph 1(a) of this Article also applies *mutatis mutandis* to States which have in matters of custody two or more systems of law of personal application.

ARTICLE 27

1. Any State may, at the time of signature or when depositing its instrument of ratification, acceptance, approval or accession, declare that it avails itself of one or more of the reservations provided for in paragraph 3 of Article 6, Article 17 and Article 18 of this Convention. No other reservation may be made.

2. Any Contracting State which has made a reservation under the preceding paragraph may wholly or partly withdraw it by means of a notification addressed to the Secretary General of the Council of Europe. The withdrawal shall take effect on the date of receipt of such notification by the Secretary General.

ARTICLE 28

At the end of the third year following the date of the entry into force of this Convention and, on his own initiative, at any time after this date, the Secretary General of the Council of Europe shall invite the representatives of the central authorities appointed by the Contracting States to meet in order to study and to facilitate the functioning of the Convention. Any member State of the Council of Europe not being a party to the Convention may be represented by an observer. A report shall be prepared on the work of each of these meetings and forwarded to the Committee of Ministers of the Council of Europe for information.

ARTICLE 29

1. Any Party may at any time denounce this Convention by means of a notification addressed to the Secretary General of the Council of Europe.

2. Such denunciation shall become effective on the first day of the month following the expiration of a period of six months after the date of receipt of the notification by the Secretary General.

ARTICLE 30

The Secretary General of the Council of Europe shall notify the member States of the Council and any State which has acceded to this Convention, of:

(a) any signature;
(b) the deposit of any instrument of ratification, acceptance, approval or accession;
(c) any date of entry into force of this Convention in accordance with Articles 22, 23, 24 and 25;
(d) any other act, notification or communication relating to this Convention.

Signatories to the Hague and European Conventions

The table below indicates those countries which are signatories to the Hague and/or European Conventions and their date of signing.

Country	Convention	Effective dates
Argentina	Hague	1/6/91
Australia	Hague	1/1/87
Austria	Hague and European	1/10/88 and 1/8/86
Bahamas	Hague	1/1/94
Belgium	European	1/8/86
Belize	Hague	1/10/89
Bosnia and Herzegovina	Hague	7/4/92
Burkina	Hague	1/8/92
Canada	Hague	1/8/86
Chile	Hague	1/5/94
Colombia	Hague	1/3/96
Croatia	Hague	1/12/91
Cyprus (Southern)	Hague and European	1/2/95 and 1/10/86
Czech Republic	Hague	1/3/98
Denmark	Hague and European	1/7/91 and 1/8/91
Ecuador	Hague	1/4/92
Federal Republic of Yugoslavia	Hague	27/4/92
Finland	Hague and European	1/8/94
France	Hague and European	1/8/86
Georgia	Hague	1/10/97
Germany	Hague and European	1/12/90 and 1/2/91
Greece	Hague and European	1/6/93 and 1/7/93
Honduras	Hague	1/3/94
Hungary	Hague	1/9/86
Iceland	Hague and European	1/10/96
Isle of Man	Hague and European	14/10/91
Israel	Hague	1/12/91
Italy	Hague and European	1/5/95 and 1/6/95
Liechtenstein	European	1/8/97
Luxembourg	Hague and European	1/7/87 and 1/8/86
Macedonia	Hague	1/12/91
Mauritius	Hague	1/6/93
Mexico	Hague	1/9/91
Monaco	Hague	1/2/93
Netherlands	Hague and European	1/9/90
New Zealand	Hague	1/8/91
Norway	Hague and European	1/4/89 and 1/5/89
Panama	Hague	1/12/91
Poland	Hague and European	1/11/92 and 1/3/96
Portugal	Hague and European	1/8/86
Republic of Ireland	Hague and European	1/10/91

Romania	Hague	1/2/93
St Kitts and Nevis	Hague	1/8/94
Slovenia	Hague	1/6/94
South Africa	Hague	1/10/97
Spain	Hague and European	1/9/87 and 1/8/86
Sweden	Hague and European	1/6/89 and 1/7/89
Switzerland	Hague and European	1/8/86
Turkmenistan	Hague	1/3/98
United Kingdom	Hague and European	1/8/86
USA	Hague	1/7/88
Venezuela	Hague	1/1/97
Zimbabwe	Hague	1/7/95

Part 2

PART

2

Algeria

■ *CONVENTIONS*

Not a signatory to the Hague or European Conventions

DOMESTIC LAW

The system is based on Islam and readers should refer to the general guide in Part 1. Article 4 of the Constitution of Algeria proclaims Islam as the State religion and the vast majority of the population are Sunni, Maliki followers. Maliki theories are the dominant principles underlying laws of personal status. To a lesser degree, later French occupation has also influenced Algeria's legal development through interpretation and administration. Regulations concerning custody are laid down in Family Law No 84 of 9 June 1984. This legislation is the country's primary source of family law and applies to Algerian nationals and foreigners resident in Algeria. Article 15 of the Civil Code states that the national law of the minor will apply in guardianship matters. Algerian children always take the nationality of their father regardless of the place of their birth, consequently, Algerian law will prevail even if the children are dual nationals. The legal profession is not divided and instructions should be transferred to an advocate who is addressed as *Maitre*.

CUSTODY

Article 65 (Family Law 84) defines custody as: 'the caring for a child, its upbringing and education in religious faith of its father, and provision for its protection, health and righteousness'. On divorce, guardianship is divided with the father acquiring sole legal guardianship or parental responsibility. Article 64 confirms that the mother has the first claim to the right of custody, that is to say the day-to-day care of the child. The next claimant under the rules of priority is the maternal grandmother, followed by the maternal aunt, the father and the paternal grandmother. Where parents reside in different countries, custody is normally granted to the father, but this does not preclude a foreign mother from gaining custody if she is resident in Algeria. Foreign parents are not prohibited from applying to the Algerian courts for custody (or access).

DURATION OF CUSTODY

Article 65 stipulates that custody will continue for boys until the age of 10. Where the custodian is his mother and she has not remarried, custody may be extended to 16 years by order of the court. Custody for girls will continue until they reach marriageable age usually considered to be around the age of 18.

ACCESS

The non-custodian parent will have the right of access and it is a criminal offence to refuse such a parent contact. To exercise this right the parent must obtain a contact order, but the applicant must be divorced before the order becomes enforceable. Access may only be taken within Algeria, although the custodian can consent to access elsewhere.

LEAVING THE JURISDICTION

Under Article 69, the party exercising custody who plans to leave Algeria to live elsewhere with the child must apply to the courts to confirm custody, thus removal requires leave of the court. Applications for leave are determined in the light of the child's interests and this includes examining the father's right of access and his supervision of other forms of guardianship. Children cannot leave the jurisdiction without the father's formal consent which must be recorded in an official document referred to as *Authorisation Paternelle de Sortie du Territoire National d'un Enfant Minuer*. This document must also be endorsed by the local police authority upon the application of the father. Irrespective of whether parents accompany their child's departure out of the country this document must be produced.

CONVENTION LAW AND PROCEDURE

Algeria is not a Convention country although there are bilateral arrangements with other States such as France.

CONTACTS

Ministry of Justice
8 Place Bir
Boite Postale 298 Hakim
El-Biar
Alger
Tel: 2 780 0290 292

Australia

■ *CONVENTIONS*
   Hague – Effective date: 1 January 1987

DOMESTIC LAW

Australia is a commonwealth of States and territories operating a common law system. Private family law is governed by federal law, except in Western Australia where State law applies.

CUSTODY

With the advent of the Family Law Reform Act, effective since 11 June 1996, all parents whether married or not have joint parental responsibility for their children. Western Australia is an exception: unmarried mothers continue to exercise guardianship and custody (ie parental responsibility and residence) alone except where there is a formal order or agreement conferring this right on the father or other persons. Consequently, unmarried fathers who are habitually resident in Western Australia who suspect that the mother may remove a child from the territory take immediate steps to obtain a court order.

Orders settling custody and access arrangements now refer to residence and contact. Orders made under the old legislation are covered by transitional provisions which convert access into contact orders and custody into residence orders. It is too early to comment on the extent to which precedents set under the old legislation will influence the interpretation of these reforms.

In non-Hague Convention cases and domestic custody hearings, the child's welfare will remain the court's paramount concern focusing attention on the child's mental, physical and financial well being. Decisions will be made in the light of long-term advantage over the short term, maintaining continuity, the existing parent–child relationship and the wishes of the child. (The weight given to a child's opinion will depend on age, maturity and the circumstances of the case.) In general, the courts will be reluctant to split siblings or separate mothers from infant children.

CONTACT

The welfare principle assumes children should grow up knowing both parents. As a result, contact will be refused only if it is clearly not in the child's interest to continue it. In difficult cases, the court is free to attach precise terms to contact orders detailing whether contact should be by telephone or post, be supervised, at certain times and/or locations, etc. If specific orders are not made, contact is intended to be frequent and regular. A court may be willing to vary any orders at a later date if it is in the child's interests to do so and circumstances are shown to have altered significantly.

The parent with whom the child resides is obliged to support contact with the other parent and encourage the child to view it positively. Failure to fulfil an order exposes the contravening party to court sanctions. Parents obstructing contact or residence may be liable to a prison sentence. Such a penalty will be imposed only if the breach is so grave that alternative penalties would be inappropriate. Consequently, a parent with residence wishing to remove the child from the jurisdiction is advised to seek the court's consent which, again, will consider the child's best interests and any change in circumstances.

WARDSHIP

Two categories of wardship exist in Australian law. State wardship is a statutory remedy committing a child into the care and protection of a State or territorial department, while court wardship places the guardianship of the child with the court and can continue until the child reaches the age of 18 years. Court wardship is now rare as the Family Court of Australia has broad statutory powers to deal with children.

FOREIGN ORDERS

Generally, there is no formal procedure for the recognition and enforcement of foreign orders. Where the Convention is not applicable, a fresh Australian residence or contact application should be made in the State or territory where the child is believed to be located. In this context, foreign orders may carry evidential weight.

LOCATING THE CHILD

When the child's whereabouts are unknown, orders may be served on the Federal and/or State police forces requiring further investigation or a warrant issued for the possession of the child. Also, the Department of Immigration, Secretary of Foreign Affairs and Trade, relevant Embassies or High Commission may be served and assistance requested. If a warrant for the possession of a child has been issued, the court may overrule secrecy regulations surrounding government records which provide information on the child's whereabouts and order searches to be undertaken by the relevant government department. If a continuous search is ordered, the department is obliged to search once every three months. Only one government department can be ordered to search at a time. Any person believed to have knowledge of the child's whereabouts can be subpoenaed and questioned by the court. Legal professional privilege will not be accepted as a reasonable excuse for failing to provide information. If the child is found, the police may conduct an initial 'safe and well' check on the child.

BORDER CHECKS

If proceedings have commenced, or a court order has been obtained, a parent may prevent the removal of a child by serving a copy of the order (if it has been made) and a statutory declaration upon international carriers, usually airlines who can be fined for ignoring notification of proceedings or an order. The Australian federal police cannot take any steps to prevent a child's departure unless provided with a copy of a court order. This will place the child on the 'Watch List' operating at points of departure. In the event that a parent or third party attempts to remove a child from the jurisdiction, the federal police have authority to hold the child. In practice, duty judges are available to make urgent orders and the police may be willing to hold a child pending receipt of the order.

PASSPORTS

Both parents, regardless of marital status, are required to give their consent prior to the issue of their child's passport. The courts have authority to dispense with the need for a parent's consent and to restrain a parent from applying or obtaining a passport for the child or themselves. At any time during proceedings, if satisfied that there is a threat that the child could be removed from Australia, the court may also order the surrender to the court of both the child's passport and the passport of other persons concerned.

Completion of a Travel Document Stop Request form issued by the Department of Foreign Affairs and Trade will warn the issuing passport authority to examine a named person's application for an Australian passport or travel document. This procedure does not cancel passports already issued nor is it an automatic guarantee that issue will be prevented and ideally it should be supported by a certified copy of the relevant court order. A 'Stop Request' can be submitted to the appropriate Australian High Commission if the primary carer is residing outside the Australian jurisdiction.

CHILD AGREEMENTS

This is a written document made between parents regarding parenting and maintenance arrangements for their children. Such agreements can affect any children. It can be drawn up outside Australia and there are no time-limits attached. Registration will render an agreement enforceable by the Family Court. This is a simple procedure which entails filing a certified copy of the agreement and an affidavit verifying it in the Family Court in the jurisdiction where enforcement is sought. The court can vary terms of the agreement if it is in the child's welfare.

CRIMINAL REMEDY

There is no specific legislation making parental child abduction a criminal offence. If a child is wrongfull removed from Australia while proceedings are pending or after a court order has been made, the courts have the power to imprison a party for up to three years. Periodic detention, fines and other sentencing alternatives may be imposed for less serious transgressions.

CONVENTION LAW AND PROCEDURE

The Hague Convention is enacted into Australian law by the Family Law (Child Abduction Convention) Regulations. Australia is a commonwealth and the following States and territories implement the Hague Convention: Australian Capital Territory, New South Wales, Northern Territory, Queensland, Victoria, South Australia, Tasmania and Western Australia. An application must be sent to the Central Authority for the Australian Commonwealth in the first instance where it will be checked to ensure Convention criteria are satisfied and documentation is correct. This process usually takes around 48 hours and, once accepted, applications are forwarded to the relevant State or territory Central Authority, ie the State or territory in which the child is believed to be located. If the child's exact location is not known, the court may issue a warrant to the police for the possession of the child (see p 64 'Locating the Child').

On receipt of a warrant, the State or territory Central Authority will assess whether it is appropriate to negotiate a voluntary return and may make the initial contact with the abducting parent as a consequence. If negotiation fails or is inappropriate, the case will be sent to the Crown Solicitor (State Lawyer) who is instructed to file the request for return (along with any required restraining orders) in the Family Court which sits in all State capitals and major towns. Direct contact between applicant and Crown Solicitor is discouraged, but may in occasional cases happen if it is deemed appropriate, otherwise all communications must go via the Central Authority. Note that, as nearly all Central Authorities are government departments whose remit is to handle every aspect of child protection, abduction resolution may be classified as non-urgent. Cases will be given priority and actioned as a matter of urgency only if a specific request is made which emphasises the likelihood of removal from the jurisdiction if the child is at risk.

Once lodged, an application for return of a child will be listed for a preliminary hearing within a short time, usually about seven days. This hearing will set a date for a defending parent to file a response and issue any necessary interim orders. It will also fix a date for the full hearing and any further interim hearings if required. The Convention hearing like all family hearings will be heard by a specialist family judge sitting alone in the first instance. It is usual practice for the court to formulate judgment using documentary evidence. Oral evidence may be required if there is a wide discrepancy in the evidence presented but the majority of applicants are not required to attend the full hearing. The court will take account of the wishes of children with sufficient maturity to understand the proceedings.

Like all family cases, Convention applications are processed expeditiously. Hearings take place in open court, but media coverage which identifies a party or person concerned with proceedings will render the reporter criminally liable. The maximum punishment for such an offence is one year's imprisonment.

HABITUAL RESIDENCE

Overall, the Australian Family Court appears to favour a slightly wider interpretation of the Convention than the English courts. Establishing a change in a child's habitual residence requires proof that both parents had a shared intention to remain in a new country. The court will also assess circumstances surrounding the geographical relocation and the passage of time since that event.

ARTICLE 12

Return orders will be mandatory if the application is made within a 12-month period which begins to run from the day of the abduction or retention and not the date the child entered Australia. The burden for substantiating settlement lies with the defending parent who must demonstrate that the child is both physically established in a new location and is emotionally settled and secure.

ARTICLE 13

The facts of a case must be of an exceptional nature for an Article 13 defence to be successfully raised and only then may the court make any welfare considerations on the child's behalf. Acquiescence must be clear and unqualified; an applicant parent must be shown to have been aware, following the child's removal or retention, that:

(1) the removal or retention was unlawful; and
(2) of his or her rights under the Convention at the time of the alleged acquiescence.

Grave physical or psychological harm must be substantial, comparable to an intolerable situation, and caused by return of the child to the applicant jurisdiction rather than the applicant parent. An applicant parent refusing to accompany a child's return will not sustain an Article 13(b) defence. However, if return would cause further problems for the child, such as a separation from siblings, or because the child is extremely young, a return order may not be made.

APPEALS

There is a right of appeal to the Appeals division of the Family Court of Australia sitting in full court (three judges) and a further right of appeal to the High Court of Australia, if the full court or the High Court has certified that there is question on a point of law to be answered.

LEGAL AID AND COSTS

Hague Convention applications are automatically funded by the Australian government and applicants are not means tested. Repatriation costs for the child and possibly for the abducting parent may have to be paid by the parent who has pursued return successfully. The Central Authority insists that overseas applicants deposit sufficient funds with their legal advisors to cover the costs of air fares, prior to processing an application through the courts. Australian applicants who do not have the financial means to pay air fares may apply for grants under the Overseas Custody (Child Removal) Scheme. Parties taking proceedings within Australia and respondents to Hague applications may engage a lawyer at their own expense and apply for legal aid. Legal aid is provided throughout Australia and this is subject to strict means and merits testing. Eligibility will depend on the criteria adopted by each state or territory. Lawyers fees are charged on a court-regulated scale of costs and the current hourly rate is Aus$117. Generally, both parties will bear their own costs in family law proceedings and orders for costs are rare.

CONTACTS

CENTRAL AUTHORITY

International Civil Procedures Section
Civil Law Division
Attorney General's Department
Robert Garran Offices
Barton ACT 2600
Tel: (61) 6 250 6724
Fax: (61) 6 250 5917

PART

2

OTHER AGENCIES

Australian Bar Association
7th Floor
Selbourne Chambers
174 Philip Street
Sydney NSW 2000

The National Council of Lawyers
19 Torrens Street
Braddon ACT 2601

Parent Support
The 'Empty Arms' Network
PO Box 4033
Auburn South
Victoria 3122
Tel: (61) 3 9882 5543
Fax: (61) 3 9882 5522
e-mail: jacq@ozemail.com.au

Canada

■ *CONVENTIONS*

Hague – Effective dates:

    Alberta 1 February 1987 English/French 001 403
    British Columbia 1 August 1986 English/French 001 604/250
    Manitoba 1 August 1986 English 001 204
    New Brunswick 1 August 1986 English/French 001 506
    Newfoundland 1 August 1986 English 001 709
    Northwest Territories 1 April 1988 English/French 001 403/819
    Nova Scotia 1 August 1986 English 001 902
    Ontario 1 August 1986 English/French
      001 416/519/613/705/807/905
    Province of Prince Edward Island 1 August 1986 English 001 902
    Quebec 1 August 1986 French 001 418/514/709/819
    Saskatchewan 1 November 1986 English 001 306
    Yukon 1 August 1986 English 001 403

DOMESTIC LAW

Canada is a federation of 12 States and territories commonly referred to as provinces. There are two sources of legislation: federal and provincial. All provinces, bar Quebec, operate legal systems founded on English common law. Quebec law is codified and, particularly in the area of civil matters, continues to be influenced by French legal principles. Lawyers in Quebec, who are able to take instructions from the client and represent them in court, are avocats and are addressed as *Maitre*. The legal profession, in the other 11 provinces, has two branches: solicitors and barristers. However, their roles are not mutually exclusive and the majority of lawyers are qualified to practice in both capacities. Practice is generally restricted to a lawyer's 'home' province. Consequently, instructions must be transferred to a practitioner in the province where the child is known, or is strongly believed, to be residing. Rights of audience extend to the Supreme Court and occasionally lawyers can obtain permission to practice out of their province. All Canadian lawyers must have membership of their provincial Bar or Law Society depending on their professional qualification.

Custody and access issues are covered by provincial family legislation and common law precedent or ancillary relief within divorce proceedings. This is regulated by the RSC 1985, a federal law applicable throughout the Canadian jurisdiction. As Canada's population is concentrated in the cities of British

Columbia, Ontario and Quebec, the probability of custody dispute and abduction is greater in these provinces. This section covers the remedies and procedures available in those jurisdictions. In British Colombia, for guardianship and custody matters, reference should be made to the Family Relations Act 1979, Chapter 128. In Ontario, corresponding legislation is found in the Children's Law Reform Act 1990, Chapter 12, and, in Quebec, in the Civil Code of Quebec S2 191 C64.

Each province administers and regulates its own court system. There is a Federal Court of Canada but it has no jurisdiction with respect to the custody and access of children except in the rarest of circumstances under the Divorce Act. Owing to its constitutional framework, a superior court judge of a general or family law trial division will make the final custody and access decisions under the federal Divorce Act 1985. Where custody and access is decided outside of the Divorce Act 1985, and pursuant to the provincial law, which varies in procedure according to the province or territory, then the decision will be made by either a superior court judge or a judge of the provincial division (ie appointed by provincial rather than federal jurisdiction). Specific reference should be made to the provincial law governing the determination of custody or access rights. There is an appeal, as a matter of right, from any final decision of first instance. There is a right of appeal, with leave to the Supreme Court of Canada, located in Canada, from any decision of the province's final court of appeal.

CUSTODY

The legal concept of 'guardianship' is equivalent to parental authority or parental rights and responsibilities. Parents of legitimate children have joint guardianship conferred on them from the birth of their child in all provinces. At common law, an unmarried mother will be the sole guardian. However, the status of unmarried fathers, in relation to guardianship, will depend on provincial legislation. In British Columbia, all parents, married or not, will share guardianship for as long as they cohabit, but where couples have separated at least six months before the birth or have never lived together the mother will be the sole guardian. This rule does not preclude an unmarried father from applying for custody or access. Ontario also recognises that unmarried mothers and fathers are both permitted to seek guardianship, and custody and access orders. The operative term in the statutes and case-law to describe the matter of parental authority or parental rights and responsibilities is that of custody. Under most of the provincial laws, parents have joint custody of their children until and unless there is a court order or an agreement specifying otherwise, or the parties separate and the child remains in the care of one parent and the other acquiesces; in that last case the de facto custody over time creates a legal entitlement. Within the past decade, all of the Canadian provinces have passed legislation, the effect of which is to abolish any differential treatment of the matter of a child's custody or access based upon the parents' marital status. There is no rule, for example, created by provincial statute, or under case-law that precludes the unmarried father from applying for and obtaining an order of sole custody.

The Divorce Act 1985 permits the courts to make custody orders concerning children of the marriage who are aged under 16 years, and when the needs of older offspring require extended arrangements. Initially, an interim order can be made once the custody application has been made. Applications from non parents may be made with the court's leave. Final orders may award sole or joint custody. When a party has sole custody the other parent has the right of access. A child will reside with the custodial parent who also has responsibility for important decisions concerning the child's upbringing and education. Under s 16(5) of the Divorce Act 1985, a parent with access becomes entitled to information relating to the child's health, education and welfare unless the terms of the order are to the contrary. This would appear to limit the right of joint guardianship previously enjoyed by the parent with access. The courts have a discretionary power to request expert evidence and to consider the wishes of older children who are deemed mature enough to express a reasoned preference. The manner in which children's evidence is heard is again left to judicial discretion, but the incorporation of the child's opinion into the report from an expert trained in child assessment is favoured practice.

In general, the Canadian courts will respect parents' mutual agreements regarding custody and access, formalising them in consent orders. The courts have the discretion to overrule such agreements or grant subsequent variation orders. Such decisions, during divorce or otherwise, must treat the child's best interest as the paramount consideration. The Divorce Act 1985 directs that reference should be made to the 'condition, means and other circumstances of the child' and past conduct relating to the ability of the parent to care for the child (s 16(8) and (9) of the 1985 Act). The Divorce Act 1985 also entrenches in s 16(10) a 'maximum contact' principle that obliges a court to consider within the test of 'best interests of the child' the comparative abilities of the parties to ensure that the child has a relationship with both parents, notwithstanding their separation.

ACCESS

A parent with access has the right to receive information about the child from third parties, such as school authorities, without the consent of the parent with custody. The right of access also gives the parent with access the entitlement to information to exercise access, including knowledge of the child's address and general routine.

CONVENTION LAW AND PROCEDURE

An application can be sent to the Federal Central Authority who will forward the application to the relevant provincial Central Authority (these are listed under the Contacts heading below). Alternatively, the application can go direct to the provincial Central Authority and it is at this stage that the application is checked to ensure Convention criteria are met and accompanying documentation is correct. Applications may be made in French or English. However, as speed is essential, an application in the language most commonly spoken may avoid unnecessary delay.

If the child's whereabouts are not known, applications must be sent via the Federal Central Authority. If there is strong evidence that a child is in a particular province, the provincial Central Authority can take the necessary steps to determine the child's whereabouts. All Central Authorities will notify the Missing Children's Registry of wrongful return or retention (the Registry's work is discussed under 'Contacts' below).

Across Canada there is no uniform Convention procedure as it is incorporated in provincial legislation. The Hague Convention covers international abductions and not those of an inter-state nature. As a general rule, the provincial Central Authority will provide the applicant with a list of lawyers who are known to have Convention experience. In Saskatchewan the Central Authority appoints a lawyer to act on behalf of the State rather than the applicant. In New Brunswick, the Crown Prosecutor, ie the State lawyer, is instructed.

Voluntary negotiated return is considered and attempted when circumstances indicate that the abducting parent is unlikely to remove the child to a third jurisdiction. However, the approach, timing and resources for this procedure will differ from province to province. If negotiations are unsuccessful, the application will be filed in the court, by way of a 'motion' or 'petition', along with a request for return and any necessary interim orders which can be applied for ex parte.

The courts will accept an applicant's affidavit evidence. Only where parties' submissions are extremely contradictory will parents be required to attend in person. The objections of a child who is mature enough to express a reasoned preference will be considered. It is common practice for an independent third party who is competent in child assessment to talk with the child and make a report. Where a child is separately represented, it is unlikely the judge will refuse to hear the child's objections in evidence.

BRITISH COLUMBIA

Once an application is accepted, the provincial Central Authority will attempt to negotiate voluntary return if appropriate. If this is unsuccessful, the Central Authority will assist the applicant in appointing a lawyer. While making the initial checks, the Central Authority will determine whether the applicant is eligible for legal aid in their home jurisdiction. If so, the applicant will be allocated a legal aid lawyer. When applicants are not eligible, they must secure legal representation privately. The Central Authority provides a list of lawyers in various areas of the province. Once a lawyer is instructed, the Central Authority will forward the application and will also continue to act in a consultancy capacity providing guidance on case-law and the Convention's procedure.

The lawyer will immediately begin proceedings by filing either a Writ of Summons and a Statement of Claim or a Petition at either the Supreme Court of British Columbia or the Provincial Court of British Columbia. Applications will normally be processed on an emergency basis. The court can make an ex parte order which prevents the abducting parent from leaving the province and/or places the child in the temporary custody of the Family and Child Services or a known third party pending the outcome of proceedings. These orders require that a further abduction has been attempted which means such requests will be made in circumstances of extreme urgency. Consequently, they can be granted verbally over the telephone by the duty judge when necessary.

Notice for the initial hearing can be as little as two days and this usually takes place in chambers. It is common for an extension of time to be granted to allow the respondent's representatives to prepare adequately. The duration of proceedings will depend on the facts of the case. In other words, the longer the child has been residing in British Columbia, the more extensive the enquiry will be. Written evidence is considered sufficient for these proceedings and an applicant is not required to attend in person. However, their presence may be useful to provide further information and facilitate a speedy return should it be ordered. An applicant parent must also expect to bear the expense of the return travel for the child and possibly for the abducting parent.

ONTARIO

The Central Authority provides a list of lawyers and will assist an applicant to secure suitably experienced legal representation. Occasionally, a Ministry of Justice solicitor will be appointed if there is an administrative or legal difficulty. An applicant may also seek legal aid by completing a financial statement form which is assessed by the Ontario Legal Aid Office but this may delay proceedings. When a parent is not eligible for legal aid, fees can be negotiated privately with a lawyer.

It is usual and encouraged practice for the Ontario-based lawyer to contact the applicant or the applicant's lawyer. Applications are filed in the civil provincial court nearest to where the child is believed to be living. Convention cases can be heard in a higher court. However, most areas of Ontario do not have a specialist family court and it is policy to apply to the local court where the judiciary are accustomed to family cases in the context of summary proceedings.

Although applications are treated expeditiously, there can be some delay, about one month, before a hearing is listed. Hearings without notice are permitted, with the leave of the court, if there is risk of a child's further removal from the jurisdiction. If the respondent is notified, the period is short, usually between five and ten days. This often leads to an adjournment to ensure the abducting parent has adequate time to instruct a lawyer. Affidavits are deemed sufficient for Convention proceedings. It is unlikely that an applicant will be obliged to attend court in person. Appeals are expedited but, even so, this procedure is lengthy, taking several months.

QUEBEC

When the whereabouts of the child are not precisely known, the Central Authority will apply via the Attorney-General to the court either to obtain permission to gather further information and question third parties or for the issue of a warrant to a police officer to inquire of the child's whereabouts and negotiate a voluntary return.

When efforts to achieve a voluntary return have failed, the Central Authority will ensure that return proceedings are immediately started in the Supreme Court of Quebec. Negotiations can continue once proceedings have begun. If they are successful, the court's approval will be sought. The Central Authority will transfer all documentation to the applicant's lawyer, provide research assistance when required and forward a legal aid application. If the parent has not already instructed a lawyer, they will be referred to the Quebec Bar Association.

An application for return may also request the grant of provisional orders which will ensure the child is not removed again.

Legal aid is provided to applicants but they must be eligible under criteria operating in Quebec law. Assessment is made by the relevant legal aid office. Sometimes a child may make their own application for legal aid if they are separately represented. Legal aid will cover the costs of fees and disbursements including those incurred by an appeal.

COSTS

All the Canadian States provide legal aid provision, but eligibility usually depends on whether the individual is eligible for legal aid in their own country. Failure to qualify in the home jurisdiction does not prevent an applicant from making a request for legal aid within Canada. The alternative for non legal aid applicants would be to arrange a reduced or contingency fee with their lawyer. Legal aid does not cover the costs of returning the child. However, the Missing Children's Registry co-ordinates a programme providing repatriation expenses for parents in need of financial assistance to collect their children. Requests should be made via the Central Authority or the police.

CRIMINAL REMEDY

Under s 282 and s 283 of the Criminal Code of Canada, parental child abduction of children under the age of 14 years is an offence. The maximum penalty if found guilty is 10 years' imprisonment. This applies to contravention of a custody order or where no custody order, joint or sole, is in place, and, in some circumstances, to instances of access denial. This federal legislation recognises that an offence has been committed if a child's presence in Canada is in breach of foreign custody orders. An offence occurs if an abduction is international, extra- or inter-provincial.

CONTACTS

FEDERAL CENTRAL AUTHORITY

Justice Legal Service (JUS)
Department of Foreign Affairs
Lester B Pearson Building, Tower C, 7th Floor
125 Sussex Drive
Ottawa, Ontario K1A 0G2
Tel: (1) 613 996 1300
Fax: (1) 613 992 6485
Telex: 053 3745

PROVINCIAL CENTRAL AUTHORITIES

ALBERTA

Alberta Justice Family Law
6th Floor, JE Brownlee Building
10365 – 97th Street
Edmonton, Alberta
T5J 3W7
Tel: (1) 403 422 3715
Fax: (1) 403 427 5914

Calgary office:
Department of Justice
Section Head, Calgary Family Law
1660 Standard Life Building
639 5th Avenue, SW
Calgary, Alberta T2P OM9
Tel: (1) 403 297 3360
Fax: (1) 403 297 6381

NEW BRUNSWICK

Attorney General of New Brunswick
PO Box 6000
Room 551, Centennial Building
Fredericton, New Brunswick
E3B 5H1
Tel: (1) 506 453 2784
Telex: (1) 0144 6230

ONTARIO

Reprocity Office
Juridiques
Ministry of the Attorney General
PO Box 640
Downsview, Ontario
M3M 3A3
Tel: (1) 416 240 2411
French speaking tel: (1) 416 240 2486
English speaking tel: (1) 416 243 1900, Ext 4130
Fax: (1) 416 240 2405

PART

2

SASKATCHEWAN

Department of Justice, Policy, Planning and Evaluation Branch
Public Law and Policy Division
1874 Scarth Street
Regina, Saskatchewan
S4P 3V7
Tel: (1) 306 787 8954
Fax: (1) 306 787 9111
Telex: 071 2586

BRITISH COLUMBIA

Ministry of Attorney General
Legal Services Branch
1301 – 865 Hornby Street
Vancouver, British Columbia
V6Z 2H4
Tel: (1) 604 660 3093
Fax: (1) 604 660 2636

NEWFOUNDLAND

Attorney General of Newfoundland
4th Floor, East Block
Confederation Building
Prince Philip Drive
PO Box 8700
St John's, Newfoundland
A1B 4J6
Tel: (1) 709 729 2887
Fax: (1) 709 729 2129

PRINCE EDWARD ISLAND

Departmental Solicitor
Department of Provincial Affairs and Attorney General
Legal Service Section
PO Box 2000, Charlottetown
Prince Edward Island
C1A 7N8
Tel: (1) 902 368 5064
Fax: (1) 902 368 4563

NORTHWEST TERRITORIES

Legal Division
Department of Justice
Government of Northwest Territories
PO Box 1320
Yellowknife, Northwest Territories
X1A 2L9
Tel: (1) 403 920 6143
Fax: (1) 403 873 0234

MANITOBA

Department of Justice
Family Law Branch
7th Floor, 405 Broadway
Winnipeg, Manitoba
R3C 3L6
Tel: (1) 204 945 2841
Fax: (1) 204 945 0053

NOVA SCOTIA

Department of the Attorney General
PO Box 7
Halifax, Nova Scotia
B3J 2L6
Tel: (1) 902 424 4044
Fax: (1) 902 424 4556
Telex: 0192 2693

QUEBEC

Direction Générale des Affaires
Ministère de la Justice du Quebec
1200 route de l'Eglise, 2e étage
Sainte-Foy, Quebec
G1V 4M1
Tel: (1) 418 644 7152
Fax: (1) 418 646 1696
English and French speakers available

YUKON

Deputy Minister of Justice
PO Box 2703
Whitehorse
Yukon
Y1A 2C6
Tel: (1) 403 667 5412
Fax: (1) 403 667 3979
Telex: 036 8260

OTHER AGENCIES

THE MISSING CHILDREN'S REGISTRY

The Missing Children's Registry was established in 1988. It is Canada's clearing-house for missing children providing investigative and consultation services to Canadian police forces and foreign police via Interpol. There is a computerised link with US law enforcement agencies. It works closely with Child Find Canada, a non-profit organisation, the Missing Children's Network and Missing Children Society of Canada. The Registry monitors and maintains a file on each missing child, receives weekly print outs from the Canadian Police Information Centre (CPIC) missing persons database which records all reported parental abductions and can make new entries regarding missing children from foreign jurisdiction believed to be in Canada. The Registry will also notify Canada's Immigration and Customs services to prevent the child's further removal.

Missing Children's Registry
c/o Royal Canadian Mounted Police
Tel: (1) 613 729 7678
Fax: (1) 613 729 6774

CHILD FIND CANADA

This is the national office of a network of independent state 'Child Find' organisations. Caseworkers meet regularly and continue to work together on casework and public awareness projects. It provides assistance in parental child abduction but its primary function is locating missing children. The organisation has good contacts with the media, police and other public services.

National Toll Free Line 800 987 7692
Child Find Canada
710 Dorval Drive, Suite 210
Oakville, Ontario
L6K 3V7
Tel: (1) 805 845 3463
Fax: (1) 905 845 9621

LE RESEAU ENFANTS RETOUR/THE MISSING CHILDREN'S NETWORK

The main concern of this organisation is tracing missing children and providing assistance in family abduction cases to parents and lawyers. It is also involved in abduction prevention, education and professional training and works alongside the media, police forces and social services.

Le Reseau Enfants Retour
The Missing Children's Network
231 St Jacques, Suite 406
Montreal, Québec
H2Y 1M6
Contact: Marcele Lamarche, Director of Search
Fax: (1) 514 843 8211

International Social Service Canada
55 Parkdale Avenue, 4th Floor
Ottawa, Ontario
K1Y 1E5
Tel: (1) 613 728 1226
Fax: (1) 613 725 0625

Missing Children Society of Canada
Suite C, 2815 – 12 Street, NE
Calgary, Alberta
T2E 7J2
Tel: (1) 403 291 0705
Fax: (1) 403 843 8211
Telex: 06367700880

Canadian Bar Association
50 O'Connor Street
Ottowa, Ontario
Tel: (1) 613 237 2925

Denmark

■ *CONVENTIONS*

Hague   – Effective date: 1 July 1991
European – Effective date: 1 August 1991

DOMESTIC LAW

Danish law is codified; legislation is developed by judicial decisions that will bind lower courts. The principle sources of family law are the Marriage Acts 1 and 2, 1969, the Children's Act 1960 which discusses paternity and the Custody Act which covers custody and access.

There is a single legal profession in Denmark whose members are referred to as *advokats*. The numbers specialising in family law are growing and the Association of Family Lawyers (address below) is well established. Matrimonial and custody proceedings, along with other civil actions, take place in the *Byretten* (the equivalent of the county court). The authority of the Bailiff's Court (or *Fogedretten*) is limited to enforcement and it does not become involved in custody decisions.

There is no specialist family judiciary, primarily because the majority of separation or divorce decrees can be obtained via a parallel administrative procedure from the County Governor, this is regarded as a quicker and cheaper system. Decisions made by the County Governor can be appealed to the Department of Private Law, while there is a right of appeal from the local court to one of two regional High Courts and thereafter to the Supreme Court.

Both procedures are covered by legal aid and family proceedings will be heard in camera. All decisions must take account of Danish law only with the consideration of the child's best interest being paramount.

NATIONALITY

An illegitimate child must take the nationality of their mother while a legitimate child can take the nationality of either parent. A child can acquire the nationality of their Danish unmarried father only on the father's subsequent marriage to the mother.

CUSTODY

Married parents will automatically hold joint parental responsibility or custody which can continue until a child reaches the age of 18 years. When a child is illegitimate the mother will retain sole parental responsibility. However, unmarried couples can agree to a shared arrangement by notifying the County Governor. Similarly, partners who are separating or divorcing may also follow this procedure to maintain joint parental responsibility. Such agreements are routinely approved by the County Governor, the exception being where an arrangement would be detrimental to the child's best interests. The County Governor will also approve arrangements where the sole custody is given to one party by mutual agreement.

When custody is disputed, couples sharing parental responsibility are first called to attend a meeting with the County Governor to reach an agreement. If this fails, one of the parties will be granted legal aid to make an application to the *Byretten* to settle sole custody on one party and the grant of access to the other.

If joint custody is to continue, the couple involved must be in agreement. The court is not permitted to make such an order unless they do so. It is current policy to encourage couples to take a conciliatory approach to resolution and s 29 of the Custody Act obliges the court (and County Governor) to offer advice and counselling via the family expert service. If an agreement is not forthcoming, one parent will be given sole custody with the other retaining rights of access. When reaching a decision, the judge may consider expert evidence. Section 29 of the Custody Act states that a judge or County Governor must discuss the wishes of children of 12 years or over without either parent being present. If an application for sole custody is made, and there is clearly a risk that the respondent could abduct a child abroad, the Minister of Justice has the discretion to grant temporary sole custody while proceedings are pending.

It is common for married couples to separate legally prior to divorce. If custody arrangements are decided during separation, it is unlikely that they will be re-examined on divorce. However, orders are varied where it can be demonstrated that a child's circumstances have changed so radically, for example, gross neglect, serious physical or mental illness, that the child's interests would merit a transfer of custody.

ACCESS

Unless a family's circumstances are exceptional, access commonly allows the non-custodial parent visitation every second weekend, two weeks during the summer and half of any other school holiday. If parents disagree on access the jurisdiction rests solely with the County Governor who is obliged by statute to offer family counselling. A custodial parent who continuously refuses to allow access may be liable to a fine. Access can be enforced via the *Fogedretten*. The persistent denial of access may also form the basis of an action in the *Byretten* for the transfer of custody.

FOREIGN PROCEEDINGS AND ORDERS

If proceedings have been instigated elsewhere, the general rule is for the Danish proceedings to be stayed, but there is an exception if an issue of parental custody is involved. Unless the jurisdiction involved is a party to one or both of the Conventions, an order will not be recognised and fresh proceedings must be brought within Denmark. Only if it can be proven that a child has been illegally (ie wrongfully) brought into Denmark will the court be compelled to hear a return application prior to making any custody decisions.

LEAVING THE JURISDICTION

Section 10(a) of the Custody Act stipulates that where parents disagree over custody both parents must give their consent for a child to leave Denmark. If there is a risk of abduction by one parent to avoid the consequence of a transfer to sole custody, s 23 of the Act permits the Ministry of Justice or County Governor temporarily to grant the other parent sole custody until an agreement or court decision, temporary or final, has been reached.

If a parent with sole custody fears abduction, they can apply to the County Governor to make access visits conditional, ie supervised, and ensure that passports are surrendered to the police or the Governor's office.

CRIMINAL REMEDY

Section 215 of the Criminal Code makes the removal of a child from the jurisdiction by one parent without the consent of the other, an offence. The abductor may receive a prison sentence of up to four years if convicted. The Danish Police will carry out an arrest on the strength of an arrest warrant issued in the UK. The Director of Public Prosecutions has the discretion to issue a 'safe-conduct' order which effectively enables an abductor to return to Denmark with the child without fear of criminal proceedings.

CONVENTION LAW AND PROCEDURE

Both Conventions are incorporated into Danish Law by Act 793 on 27 November 1990, known as the Abduction Act. This legislation is not applicable to the territories of the Faroe Islands or Greenland. The Central Authority is the highest administrative authority for family disputes in Denmark. On receipt, the Central Authority checks all applications to ensure they meet Convention criteria and the correct documentation is attached. They are then translated into Danish and forwarded directly to the *Fogedretten* in the area where the child is believed to be. This is a civil court dealing specifically with enforcement proceedings. Where the child's whereabouts are not known, the Central Authority can simply request assistance from the police (*Politiets Eftersøgningstjeneste*) to investigate further. A court order is not required.

If appropriate, the court will arrange a meeting with the abductor to negotiate voluntary return, and proceedings may be postponed for up to one month to allow time for a return. Once it is clear that this procedure has failed, the court will immediately continue proceedings and can appoint a lawyer on the applicant's behalf if necessary.

Alternatively, an applicant may wish to instruct a lawyer with child abduction experience direct, who will lodge the return application with the relevant *Fogedretten*. This must be submitted in Danish. Convention cases are given priority and the first hearing, ordering the abductor to attend court, is listed within a few weeks of filing.

There is no requirement for the respondent to give a written response prior to the initial hearing, at which the *Fogedretten* will consider any foreign return orders and whether the removal was wrongful. The court has the discretion to dismiss an application or postpone proceedings to allow the respondent adequate time to prepare evidence. Interim orders will be issued to prevent the child's removal from the jurisdiction and to safeguard satisfactory care arrangements pending the outcome of a full hearing which may entail the child being taken into the care of social services. It is unlikely that an applicant will be required to give evidence in person at this stage. However, their attendance may avoid the involvement of a third party in the child's care. Documents and affidavits will require translation into Danish. The interval between interim and full hearing is usually two to three months depending on the circumstances surrounding the case.

DEFENCES

ARTICLE 12

The 12-month period will begin to run from the date the child left the jurisdiction of habitual residence or the date the child should have been returned. An applicant will not be disqualified because they gave consent for an access visit to be extended. If an abductor has remained in hiding with the child, the court is likely to decide that resettlement has not been established. However, if an applicant has failed to instigate proceedings for any other reason than that the child's location was unknown it is probable the court will dismiss a return request.

ARTICLE 13(b)

When a defence under Article 13(b) is raised, the court is obliged to consider expert opinion. It is insufficient for the respondent to argue that the child is thriving in its new environment nor would a claim of previous 'ruthless conduct' by an applicant be satisfactory. A return will be refused if it can be demonstrated that the child is 'almost certain to suffer harm after return'.

ARTICLE 13(c)

Danish legislation does not clarify the age at which it is appropriate for a child to express its objections to return under Article 13(c). In practice, it is accepted that the views of older children will carry greater weight and the court will be strongly influenced by s 29 of the Majority Act which directs a judge making a custodial decision to discuss the wishes of a child who has reached the age of 12 years.

If a return order is given, the court may stipulate how the return should be conducted; for instance, the child may be placed in the care of a social worker prior to their collection by the applicant or the respondent may agree to accompany the child's return to its habitual residence. Most decisions from the Bailiff's Court are appealed in either one of Denmark's two regional High Courts whose jurisdictions are divided geographically into 'east' and 'west' and are referred to as the *Østre Landsret* and *Vestre Landsret* respectively. Thereafter, an appeal may travel to the Supreme Court or *Hojesteret*. An appeal will postpone the execution of the return order.

COSTS AND LEGAL AID

Until legal aid is granted, parents can contact a Danish lawyer direct and negotiate a fee, but the assistance given by the Central Authority is usually sufficient, and cost free. Legal aid or *fri proces* is granted to foreign non-residents, but this is subject to a means test. Applicants with an annual income of 185,000 Danish Crowns (DC) or less will be eligible, those who are married or cohabiting will be successful if joint income is 234,000 DC or less. For each child under 18 living with or supported by the applicant, the amount is raised by 32,000 DC. Legal aid will cover all costs and the grant of legal aid to pay for travel costs to attend hearings has been known. In urgent cases, there is emergency legal aid provision.

Applications will be processed by the court. However, Denmark is a party to the 1977 European Agreement on the Transmissions of Applications for Legal Aid (see p 11). It is accepted practice for the court to allocate a 'legal aid' lawyer on the client's behalf but, if the parent has already instructed a representative, the court will be willing to accept this appointment as long as the lawyer involved also participates in the legal aid scheme.

Parents must expect to bear the costs of their child's repatriation themselves if they are successful in obtaining a return order. Clients who are not eligible for legal aid will have to pay for a lawyer's services privately; the usual hourly rate is £120.

PART 2

CONTACTS

CENTRAL AUTHORITY

Ministry of Justice
Department of Private Law
(Civilretsdrektoratet)
Aebelagade 1
2100 Copenhagen O
Tel: (45) 33 92 3302
Fax: (45) 39 27 1889

OTHER AGENCIES

The Danish Bar and Law Society
Kronprinsessegade 28
DK – 1006 Copenhagen K
Tel: (45) 33 37 92 00 Kvaesthusgade 3

Ministry of Justice
Slotsholmsgade 10
DK 1216 Copenhagen K
Tel: (45) 33 92 33 40

The Association of Family Lawyers
FAF Farimagsgade 65
Att: Advokat Sys Rovsing Koch
Norksker & Jacoby
Kvaesthusgade 3
DK – 1251 Copenhagen K
Tel: (45) 33 11 08 85

Legal Aid
Københavns Statsamt
Nannasgade 28
DK – 3300 Copenhagen N
Tel: (45) 31 85 42 00

Egypt

- *CONVENTIONS*
  None

DOMESTIC LAW

The system is based on Islam and readers should refer to the general guide in Part 1.

Ninety per cent of Egypt's population are Muslim, the majority of whom are members of the Maliki and/or Shafii sect. The remainder are Christian who are mostly Coptic. There is no declaration within the Egyptian Constitution that Islam is the State religion or the country is a religious State. However, subsequent amendment to Article 2 affirms Sharia principles as the chief source of Egyptian law. Consequently, where statute remains silent there is recourse to classical Sunni Islamic theories.

The legal profession is not divided; members are advocates who are addressed as *Maitre*. Rights of audience in different courts accumulate as an advocate gains experience. Junior lawyers undertaking their practical two-year training period may appear in the Summary Courts and Courts of First Instance, after which they may practice in their own right. After three years, a lawyer can appear in the High Court of Appeal. Senior advocates with no less than seven years practice may be allocated rights to appear in the Supreme Court.

Personal status legislation has selected principles from all four Sunni schools of jurisprudence and all Egyptian nationals who are Muslims are subject to it. Article 16 of the Civil Code stipulates that the nationality of the minor determines the applicable law in matters of guardianship. Children of Egyptian fathers will be deemed Egyptian, hence Egyptian law will apply. Issues of personal status are regulated by Law No 100/1985 which amends Law No 25 of 1929 and revives, almost entirely, Law No 44 of 1979 which was declared unconstitutional. Article 20 specifies the duration and the order of claims to custody. Jurisdiction for guardianship and custody claims rest with the Summary Courts, which are the approximate equivalent of district or magistrates' courts. Applications are heard by a judge sitting alone. Decisions on unsettled claims and appeals are taken by the Courts of First Instance, located in the regional centres, by a panel of three judges.

CUSTODY

On divorce or separation, the mother will have the prior claim to custody. In general terms, the order of claim passes to female family members, preference is given to closer relations and those related to the mother over the father. Thereafter, male relatives will have a right to claim. Foreign parents are entitled to make applications for custody or access.

Custody will be forfeited should a custodial mother choose to remarry or relocate to place which would prevent the father having access or undertaking his supervisory duties. This precludes a mother from taking the child out of the Egyptian jurisdiction without the father's permission. A father can travel with the child during the period of custody.

DURATION OF CUSTODY

A woman's right to exercise custody terminates when boys reach the age of 10 and girls reach 12. However, custody may continue until a boy reaches 15 and a girl is married if a judge deems it to be in the minor's interests. A non-Muslim mother may be disqualified or have the duration of custody limited in order to safeguard the child's proper religious education.

ACCESS

The parent without custody is entitled to access. Grandparents also have this right if the parent in question is not available. If access is disputed, arrangements can be formalised by the court. If access continues to be unenforceable the custodian will receive a judicial warning. When further non-compliance occurs an enforceable order will be made and the custodian will be dismissed for a specific period and another custodian (usually the person with the next claim to custody) will be appointed.

CONVENTION LAW AND PROCEDURE

Egypt is a non-convention country. The courts will consider the final order of a competent foreign court if it is placed before them. Where there is no bilateral treaty, regard will be given as to whether there is an established comity between the two countries, whether the order conforms to Egyptian public policy or morality, whether there is conformity with the laws of the originating jurisdiction and whether the parties have been summoned properly.

CONTACTS

Ministry of Justice
Lazoughly Square
Sayeda Zeinab
Cairo
Tel: (00) 202 355 1176

Syndicate of Lawyers
Abdelkhalek Street
Cairo
Tel: (00) 202 575 2131 or (00) 202 575 2335

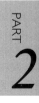

PART

2

France

■ *CONVENTIONS*

Hague – *Effective date: 1 August 1986*
European – *Effective date: 1 August 1986*

DOMESTIC LAW

Family law is set down in Articles 144 to 487 of the Civil Code (for guidance on procedure refer to the third book of the Code of Civil Procedure). Although case-law is not regarded as binding, it is extremely influential and decisions are reported in legal reviews.

Family proceedings (and correspondence between lawyers) are confidential. Cases are heard before a family judge and take place in the *tribunal de grande instance*. Being the lowest tier in France's decentralised court hierarchy, there are over 180 *tribunaux* in France. The defendant's residence will determine the appropriate jurisdiction. There is a right of appeal to one of 35 regional appeal courts (*Cour d'Appel*) and further appeals on points of law may be made to the Court of Cassation (*Cour de Cassation*) which is the highest court and sits in Paris.

All lawyers are attached to a local Bar association referred to as *Ordres des Avocats*. Instructions should always be directed to an *avocat* who has rights of audience at a hearing. However, representation on appeal must be handled by an *avoué*.

CUSTODY

Parental rights and duties or parental authority (*autorité parentale*) over a child is automatically vested jointly in parents on the birth of a legitimate children. Unmarried parents also have joint parental authority if the father recognises paternity and cohabits with the mother pursuant to the law dated 8 January 1997. Custody disputes and divorce proceedings also settling custody are handled in the *tribunal de grande instance*. The court can take account of wishes of children who are old enough to understand the proceedings (Law 8 January 1997). It is customary for joint parental authority to continue while one parent is awarded custody unless this is deemed to be contrary to the child's interests. A non-custodial parent will retain access rights and the right to influence major decisions affecting the child. Parents are free to seek the variation of an order if a change in circumstance has occurred.

APPOINTING A CHILDREN'S LAWYER

Neither parent is permitted to engage a lawyer on their child's behalf. To ensure an appointment is neutral, the President of the Bar in the region the case is to be heard makes the appointment. The child will be allocated a legal aid lawyer who will then make contact with the child. In Paris, there is a designated group of specially trained lawyers who represent children in both criminal and civil proceedings called the 'Antennae for Minors'.

EMERGENCY ORDERS

Référé proceedings are instigated by an *assignation en référé*, which is similar to an emergency writ of summons, ordering the abductor to appear before the family judge usually within a period of 15 days. In cases of extreme urgency, where a long waiting period can be shown to be detrimental, for example where there is a likelihood of re-abduction or a child needs to register for school, a *référé d'heure à heure* should be requested. This order can allow a hearing to take place within a matter of hours. Information substantiating the special reason for applying for a *référé d'heure à heure* should be on file and made available to the court. Although the *Procureur* will have only a limited authority to intervene, he or she must be notified and served with the *assignation en référé* and evidence.

A parent with joint parental authority may not remove the child from France without the other parent's consent. An order prohibiting a removal may be applied for.

BORDER CHECKS

Parents who have refused consent to the removal of their child from France and suspect that a removal is likely to occur should register their refusal with air and border police who will endeavour to stop the child from leaving the jurisdiction.

BILATERAL TEATIES

Bilateral treaties exist with Algeria, Morocco and Tunisia. Under the agreement with Algeria, the correct forum to settle custody regarding children of married Franco–Algerians is deemed to be the country where the matrimonial home was established. Both Morroco and Tunisia have agreed

PART **2**

to recognise and enforce existing French orders and when necessary return the child to France.

CRIMINAL OFFENCE

Under Article 227 of the Penal Code, parental child abduction is recognised as an offence punishable with up to one years' imprisonment and a heavy fine. If information with regard to the child's whereabouts is withheld and the child is taken out of France, this penalty may be doubled. Similarly, it is an offence to withhold access rights from a person with parental authority.

CONVENTION LAW AND PROCEDURE

Policy favours the use of the Hague Convention for bringing about a child's return rather than extraditing the abductor which is a far lengthier procedure.

On receipt, the Central Authority will check that the application satisfies Convention criteria and that it is accompanied by the correct documentation. The case is forwarded to the public prosecutor (*Procureur de la République*) attached to the civil court of first instance known as the *tribunal de grande instance* in the local jurisdiction in which the child is located. Alternatively, the petitioning parent is free to instruct a local lawyer to apply to the relevant tribunal for an emergency order known as a *référé*, (see 'Emergency Orders' below). Bypassing the Central Authority will save time, but the *Procureur*'s service will not be available and a local lawyer will be required whose experience with Convention cases must be verified.

When the child's whereabouts are unknown, the *Procureur* can ask for *police judiciaire* to investigate further. Such help will not be so easily obtainable if a parent exercises their option to seek a *référé*. Initially, the *Procureur* will contact an abductor to negotiate a voluntary return or resumption of access. If this fails, formal proceedings are begun by serving the abductor with a writ to appear in court. The hearing date will depend on the work-load of the tribunal in question; applicants may have to wait for a period of two or three months if a court has a heavy backlog. The delay may also be extended due to the necessity for the public prosecutor to proceed to an enquiry. A specialised judge *Judge aux affaires familiales* will hear the case. The same judge will sit alone if an application is felt to be straightforward and a *référé* may be ordered. Pleadings and evidence can be filed at any time prior to the hearing. A petitioner should be aware that late filing by the defendant could force them to request an adjournment. These proceedings are termed JAF proceedings and are intended to be informal. This may give a parent the opportunity to talk to the court. Traditional rules of evidence do not consider a parent an objective witness, court decisions being based on assessments of affidavits from third parties. Parents wishing to attend should not expect to be cross-examined and they should be prepared to cover the costs of an interpreter. If they are on legal aid, a translator may be appointed by the judge. Consequently, this limits the influence a parent may have on proceedings and reinforces the need for the home lawyer to provide assistance by collecting evidence to demonstrate that the child's return is desirable and pre-empt any argument citing Article 13(b).

DEFENCES

For a defence under Article 13(b) to be successfully raised, evidence of the applicants behaviour or living conditions must be extremely negative. The court will consider the wishes of children, generally from the age of 10 or 11 years old, which judges refer to as the 'age of understanding'. These children are assisted by their own *avocat* (see 'Appointing a Children's Lawyer' above). Prior to the hearing, the child's lawyer (who will always be appointed on legal aid), will have talked to the child to ascertain the child's true wishes. The child's lawyer may not communicate with parents unless the child's wishes cannot be determined and an out-of-court agreement requires negotiation or the parents' consent for an expert to be appointed to help determine the child's wishes. The judge will hear the child separately with only the child's lawyer present. If the judge is not satisfied that the child understands its own wishes then an expert's report can be ordered.

The court is not obliged to ensure that a judgment is immediately enforceable. Decisions are appealable to the *Cour d'Appel*, a procedure which can take several months.

COSTS AND LEGAL AID

The *Procureur de la République* is a civil servant and appears in court on behalf of the State and not the applicant parent. Hence, no fee will be incurred for this service. However, a parent instructing a local lawyer will be charged, although they may qualify for legal aid which will entail an assessment of income, dependants and capital. France has signed the European Agreement for the Transmission for Legal Aid (see p 11 for further details). Claimants who are not habitually resident in contracting states to this agreement must apply in French to the Legal Aid office attached to the relevant *tribunal de grande instance* or the Paris bureau. Evidence of income and expenses such as rent, insurance etc are to be communicated along with a special form for means testing.

CONTACTS

CENTRAL AUTHORITY

Ministère de la Justice
Bureau de l'Entraide
Judiciare Internationale
13 Place Vendôme
75042 Paris Cedex 01
Tel: (33) 1 44 861 466
Fax: (33) 1 44 861 406

OTHER AGENCIES

Ministère de la Justice
13 Place Vendôme
75001 Paris
Tel: (33) 1 44 77 60 60

Ordre des avocats (Paris Bar)
Palais de Justice
Boulevard du Palais
75001 Paris
Tel: (33) 1 44 32 48 48
Fax: (33) 1 44 34 77 65

Association pour la promotion de la médiation famille
Espace 15
14 rue des Frères Morane
75015 Paris

Women Living Under Muslim Laws
Femmes Sous Lois Musulmanes
Boite Postale 23
34790 Grabels
Montpellier

Legal Aid (Paris Office)
Bureau d'aide juridictionelle
Tribunal de grand instance
4 Boulevard du Palais
75001 Paris
Tel: (33) 1 44 32 47 71

Association des Avocats de la Famille

Collectif de Solidarité aux mères des familiale enfants enlevés
6 Place Saint-Germain des Près
75006 Paris
Contact: Odette Brun
Tel: (33) 1 45 34 49 10

Germany

■ *CONVENTIONS*

Hague – *Effective date: 1 December 1990*
European – *Effective date: 1 February 1991*

DOMESTIC LAW

The Fourth Book of the Civil Code provides the basis of German family law. Custody matters may be affected by old East German law if custody was vested in a parent prior to reunification in 1990. The civil law commentary is the *Palandt* which every judge and attorney will have and refer to. This also holds all the necessary information on the Hague Convention.

On 1 July 1998, German civil law was substantially revised, in that unmarried fathers are now entitled to rights of custody.

CUSTODY

Parental custody (*elterlich Sorge*) is jointly held by a married couple from the birth of their child until he reaches majority at the age of 18. So far as the children of unmarried parents are concerned, there are two ways by which the father can now acquire rights of custody:

(a) if the parents jointly declare before a notary that they wish to have joint custody (s 1676aI1 of the German Civil Code); or

(b) if the parents marry after the child is born (s 1676aI2, ibid).

During and after divorce, custody disputes (between parents) are settled by the *Amtsgericht* (local court), whilst it was common practice for the court to award one parent custody over the other parent during divorce. Under the revised law, it is the norm for the parents to continue to have joint custody, and sole custody orders will only be made where this is demonstrably in the child's best interests. The parent from whom custody has been removed will still retain the right of contact. However, continued dispute may cause access to be restricted to prevent the child being exposed to further conflict.

CHILDREN'S VIEWS

The German courts have developed a practice of taking into account children's views. Section 1671 of the Civil Code does not itself resolve whether or not the court is required to take into account the views of a child, in that it does not set out a procedural approach. However, s 50bII of the Law of Non-Contentious Matters provides that, where children are aged 14 years and over, the court is required to take that child's views into account. In the case of younger children, there is a discretion. It is important to note that s 50bII applies to domestic custody cases, but not to those brought under the Hague Convention. Thus, in a Hague case, the mandatory distinction for 14-year-olds and over does not apply. Finally, pursuant to the general principle enshrined in the constitution of the Federal Republic of Germany, a court will hear a child of any age.

FOREIGN ORDERS

When the European Convention (or any other Convention) is not available, there is a special procedure (cf s 328 of the *Zivilprozessordnung* (ZPO) Code of Civil Procedure) which should be followed to allow a German court to acknowledge a foreign order and declare it executable.

PASSPORTS

The German authorities will not issue a minor's passport unless both parents have authorised it. However, a minor's passport will be issued to a parent with sole custody of the minor, therefore the other parent's consent is not required to remove a child from the jurisdiction.

EXIT BAN

If a child's removal is anticipated, a contact parent or parent with shared custody may petition the *Amtsgericht* for the limitation or transferral of rights where the custodial parent can be shown to be misusing their rights of custody by removing the child. An exit ban should be requested simultaneously forbidding the child's removal abroad. This can be put into effect quickly by a provisional order and the Frontier Protective Direction should be informed by sending an executed decree. Interpol will then be notified. However, with the relaxation of customs laws within the EU, it is questionable how effective a ban will be because frontier checks, at their best, are infrequent.

CRIMINAL REMEDY

The removal of a child is a criminal offence punishable by up to five years' imprisonment or a fine. However, the current policy of the public prosecutor and police alike is to regard parental abduction as a domestic dispute. If a parent wishes to pursue a prosecution, an application must be made within three months of the abduction. Although German Interpol can be involved in the search for a child, foreign arrest warrants require special proceedings to ensure that they will be recognised and thus enforceable.

CONVENTION LAW AND PROCEDURE

Germany's Central Authority, which is part of the Federal Public Prosecutor's department, will take a parent's direct application as well as those from other appropriate Central Authorities. It is advisable to file the request in German using, if possible, a German application form. Attached documents should also be translated to avoid delay. On receipt, the application is checked to ensure it satisfies Convention criteria and, if accepted, given a docket number.

If the abductor's address, or likely address, is known, the abductor will be notified in writing of the legal obligation to return the child under the Hague Convention and to reply to the Central Authority within five working days. If a response is forthcoming, the Central Authority will endeavour to negotiate a voluntary return. For contact applications, youth welfare officers are asked to provide information on a child's living conditions prior to any negotiation. If the abductor's whereabouts are not known, the Central Authority will ask the Federal Public Prosecutor to take all necessary steps to locate them. Tracing an abductor or third party is facilitated by German law which requires everyone to register their change of residence within three weeks. However, non-registration is a minor offence and further investigation may be required.

If negotiations fail, or the waiting period expires, the application will be filed with the family department of the local court or *Amtsgericht* closest to the abductor's location, along with a request for legal aid. The form of request is simple; it should list the parties involved, the court's correct address and contain the requirements for return as identified by Article 3 of the Hague Convention. Further time is saved by making the request direct to the court rather than waiting for the Central Authority to do so.

Although legal representation is not mandatory, it is wise to instruct a German lawyer at this point. The *Amtsgericht* may allocate an attorney, but the IAF, local bar associations, professional bodies and the Central Authority (see below) can also provide referrals. Finding an experienced abduction attorney is a priority; instructions can be delegated to a local lawyer if attendance is required at any preliminary hearings.

It is *Amtsgericht* policy to act promptly, usually within a few days to two weeks. Once the judge has filed the request, another docket number will be assigned, the abductor or respondent will be served with a copy of the request and asked to reply in a short time. It is also usual for a hearing date to be set. Investigation and hearing procedure is inquisitorial, thus the judge will prepare the case using his discretion to make relevant directions to the police and social services, request documentation and call witnesses. It is common for these hearings to be brief, but it is advisable for parents to attend in person. An order will be made for return or dismissing the application which is effective when parents are notified. Further orders to facilitate the return may be attached, such as the surrender of passports or arrest. The order, which is written, will be accompanied by an explanation of the judge's decision. This will allow an attorney to evaluate whether a parent may appeal. Right of appeal is to the *oberlandesgricht* (Court of Appeal) which is organised on a regional basis.

Germany operates a decentralised court hierarchy of which the *Amtsgericht* is the lowest tier. Decentralisation has prevented clear case-law from developing and experience indicates that the German interpretation of the Conventions is less rigorous than in other signatory States.

COSTS AND LEGAL AID

Overall, costs are relatively cheaper compared to those in other countries, although a specialist lawyer's charges are likely to be higher. Charges depend on the value of the case which is set by the court. Hourly rates are rarely charged but may be arranged via a special agreement termed *Honorarvereinbarung*. For example, a custody case could cost 5000 DM, the attorney's fee being valued at 598 DM and is inclusive of 15 per cent sales tax. Additional administration costs (up to 40 DM), travel expenses and compensation for time spent absent from an office (between 20 DM and 75 DM per day, and if abroad this is increased by 50 per cent) are chargeable.

Germany has made a reservation on Article 26. However, means-tested legal aid (*Prozesskostenhilfe*) is available and net income, property and dependants will be factors considered when eligibility is assessed. Net income is the figure reached after taxes, national insurance and rent are deducted. Claimants are allowed no more than 649 DM per month with an allowance of 456 DM per child to qualify. The Ministry of Justice revises these rates yearly. Applications are made by the Central Authority to the *Amstergerichte* on the parent's behalf. A parent should make their request to the Central Authority for legal aid by fax, in German, using the correct pro forma.

CONTACTS

CENTRAL AUTHORITY

Der Generalbundesanwalt beim
Bundesgerichtshof-Zentrale
Behorde nach dem Häägerkindesentführungsübereinkornung unt Europäl-
schen Sorgerechtsubereinkommens – Ausfuhrungsgesetz
Neuenburgerstrasse 15
10969 Berlin
Tel: (49) 30253880
Fax: (49) 3025388397

OTHER AGENCIES

IAF (*Interessengemeinschaft der mit Auslandern verheirateten Frauen*) is a
national association for bi-national marriages, families and partnerships.
Organised from Frankfurt, it has 45 regional groups providing a variety of
services from counselling to social activities. The IAF is conversant and
involved with the issue of child abduction and a parent needing support
should contact them. The organisation has links internationally and with the
German legal profession, social services, the police and voluntary sector in
general and is a useful source of referral.

IAF – Verband bi-nationaler Familien und Partnerschaften
Ludofusstrasse 2-4
60487 Frankfurt
Contact Doris Pfeiffer-Pandey, Social Worker
Tel: (49) 69 7 07 50 87
     (49) 69 7 07 50 88
Fax: 069 7 07 50 92

Ministry of Justice
Bundesministerium der Justiz
Heinemannstrasse 6
D 53175 Bonn

Ministry of Youth
Bundesministerium fur Frauen und Jugend
Rochustrasse 8-10d
D 53113 Bonn

(Professional Body)
Bundesrechtanwaltskammer
Joachimstrasse 1
D 53113 Bonn
Tel: (49) 228 223 005
Fax: (49) 228 261 538

Frontier Protection Direction
Grenzschutzdirektion
Postfach 1644
5400 Koblenz
Tel: (49) 261 399 250
Fax: (49) 261 399 218

Internationaler Sozialdeinst
Deutscher Zweig EV
AM Stockborn 5–7
60439 Frankfurt/Main

(Family Judges and Attorneys Association)
Deutscher Familiengerichstag
Balthasa Neumann-Platz 3
D 50321 Bruhl

(National Association of Lawyers)
Deutscher Anwaltverein
Adenauerallee 106
D 53113 Bonn

Greece

- **CONVENTIONS**

  Hague – *Effective date: 1 June 1993*
  European – Effective date: 1 July 1993

DOMESTIC LAW

The principles of family law are set down in Book IV of the Civil Code. Radical reforms were introduced during the 1980s, the most important being L.1329/1983. This legislation expunged traditional patriarchal doctrine and modernised parental rights and duties. Decisions on international child abduction are published in the *Harmenopoulos* (Monthly Law Review) edited by the Thessaloniki Bar Association, and other Greek law reviews.

The legal profession is not divided and all members are referred to as attorneys. Attorneys' rights of audience are initially limited to the district courts in their region. After four years, they may appear in the Court of Appeal and after eight years, in the Supreme Court. There is no professional organisation of family attorneys although many do specialise in family law.

The court system does not accommodate family cases into a specialised court. The Court of First Instance is the district civil court with a right of appeal on facts and law to a Court of Appeal sitting in one of the 13 largest cities. Further appeal is possible to the Supreme Court in Athens on points of law only.

CUSTODY

Married couples will automatically have the right to exercise parental care which entails the right to the child's custody and the obligation to safeguard the child's physical and mental welfare. All decisions must be mutually agreed and taken in the child's best interests. An unmarried mother exercises parental care alone and this cannot be altered by an acknowledgement of paternity either voluntarily or judicially. However, the parents' subsequent marriage will do so. A child will be deemed a Greek national if either parent is Greek, but being born of non-Greek parents in Greece does not confer nationality.

On divorce or separation, parents may settle custody between themselves. If they cannot agree or existing arrangements break down, either party may apply to the district civil court. Article 1511 of the Civil Code obliges the court to make decisions without discriminating against a parent on the grounds of gender or nationality. A judgment will be given only if it is in the child's interests to do so. The majority of couples will continue to hold the right of parental care jointly. However, the right to exercise parental care will be restricted to the parent with whom the child is to live.

A residential parent is permitted to take independent decisions regarding the child's daily care, but both parents must agree on important matters such as education, medical treatment and the child's departure from the jurisdiction. Only in an emergency can one parent act alone. If parents cannot reach a decision, they should return to the court for adjudication. Thus, parents unable to agree to a child leaving the jurisdiction must return to court for formal consent and demonstrate that the child's departure from Greece is in his interest. Similarly, the courts reserve the right to overturn or modify undertakings given to the High Court in England and Wales where children have been returned to Greece under the Hague Convention.

The non-residential parent retains the right of access and the court may stipulate conditions for contact with regard to supervision, location or whether it should be direct or via telephone, etc. Arrangements can be altered if circumstances change and it is possible for a parent to regain the right to exercise parental care. In extreme situations, the court can remove the right of parental care altogether. If this occurs, it is irrevocable and the excluded parent retains no rights. Primary consideration is given to the child's best moral and material interests and the court will be mindful of existing arrangements, maintaining continuity for the child and the child's own wishes.

PASSPORTS

The issue of a passport to a minor requires the consent of both parents unless parental authority and/or custody of the minor has been awarded by the court to one parent only. If this has occurred, the parent who retains these rights has sufficient authority to consent to the issue of a child's passport. This parent also has the right to request the surrender of a current passport and prevent the issue of any subsequent passports. Such requests should be addressed to the competent Public Prosecutor.

BORDER CHECKS

There is a procedure enabling a parent with custodial rights to prevent the removal of a child by the non-custodial parent or third party. Its instigation requires a prior order from a Public Prosecutor before the police can act. This is in the form of a 'Warning to Police Authorities' at all points of exit containing a request to intercept the child's departure. Such an order requires evidence that the removal is wrongful, ie

- contrary to the applicant's custody rights;
- the threat is real and imminent; and
- the removal will take the child beyond the Greek jurisdiction.

The prosecutor will assess the request and supporting evidence on an emergency basis. A parent can also lodge a petition to the nearest member of a Court of First Instance requesting provisional measures preventing removal. However, a 'Warning' from a Prosecutor is the more effective of the two remedies.

CRIMINAL REMEDY

Parental child abduction is recognised as an offence. Greece will apply a foreign warrant of arrest only if an extradition treaty exists with the other country and the subject of the warrant is a non-Greek.

CONVENTION LAW AND PROCEDURE

Applications must be made via the Greek Central Authority. The provision of applications and accompanying documentation translated into Greek is strongly recommended. Once checked to ensure that Convention criteria are satisfied, the application is forwarded to the Public Prosecutor, via the local office of the Ministry of Justice, in the area the child is believed or known to be. If the child cannot be located, the police will be asked to investigate further. The defendant parent is contacted and an interview is arranged to negotiate for the child's voluntary return.

If this action fails, the Prosecutor will file the application with the clerk of the district civil court who will set a date for the first hearing. An interim order may also be requested at the same time to ensure the child remains in Greece pending the outcome of proceedings. A hearing should follow within a few weeks, taking place in one of 63 district courts before a panel of three judges, or, more commonly, one judge sitting alone. Pleadings can be filed at any time prior to the first hearing save in exceptional circumstances. Further evidence can be introduced with leave of the court. Proceedings are adversarial and the judiciary, who are authorised to conduct investigations, may consider any resulting evidence along with that presented in court. The court is considered to interpret Article 13(b) of the Convention rather broadly; reports by social workers and the child's wishes are given serious consideration.

As with all family proceedings, Convention hearings are open to the public and the media will have access. However, where a judge seeks the child's opinion, he has the discretion to order a closed court. Judgments are given approximately three weeks after the hearing closes and may be appealed.

A relatively recent signatory, Greece has met some criticism regarding its implementation of the Hague Convention. The statutory emphasis on procedure over substantive issues has been identified as a major source of difficulty. Safeguarding the child's speedy return is a prominent feature of the Convention. Such a concern compels applicants to pursue provisional remedies obtainable from the district court rather than final judgment via the more lengthy normal procedure. Where a provisional remedy is sought, evidence satisfying a burden of proof on the balance of probability is required by the court. However, for full orders, proof must be persuasive, ie clear and convincing, and formal methods of presenting evidence must be observed. The Greek courts have taken the view that international abduction is a dispute which merits final judgment rendering provisional orders open to appeal. The appeal process may continue for a number of years giving time for children to resettle and making a return contrary to their interests. Practitioners need to be aware of this predicament when instructing their Greek colleagues.

COSTS AND LEGAL AID

Greece has made an amendment to Article 26 of the Hague Convention which restricts payment of Greek attorney's fees to amounts equivalent to legal aid rates. Lawyers are willing to negotiate contingency fees and such agreements may be filed with the local Bar Association. Lawyers' fees will vary depending on the complexity of a case. It would be reasonable to expect a 'Bill of Services' for between £1,500 to £2,000 for representation in the Court of First Instance and in the Appeal Court. Services from lawyers employed by the Greek State are free of charge.

Greece does not operate a legal aid system but minimal provision referred to as 'benefits of property' is available. This is means-tested. Applicants must demonstrate that the payment of legal expenses would render them unable to support their own and their family's basic needs. Foreign applications are accepted if reciprocal arrangements are in place. Greece is a signatory of the 1977 European Agreement on the Transmission of Applications for Legal Aid (see p 11). Applications should be made in Greek and are assessed by the judge hearing the case. Any forthcoming assistance will not cover the child's travel costs if a return is ordered.

CONTACTS

CENTRAL AUTHORITY

Ministère de la Justice
Direction de l'élaboration des Lois
4ème Section
Athens
Tel: (30) 1 771 4186
Fax: (30) 1 770 7025

OTHER AGENCIES

Athens Bar Association
60 Akadimias Street
106 79 Athens
Tel: (30) 1 36 14 189; (30) 1 36 14 290

Athens District Court
Scholi Sokratous Street
104 31 Athens
Tel: (30) 1 32 47 494

Thessaloniki Bar Association
Dikastiko Megaro
Thessaloniki
Tel: (30) 31 528 762

Courts of Thessaloniki
Dikastiko Megaro
Thessaloniki
Tel: (30) 31 522 021

India

PART

2

- **CONVENTIONS**
  None

DOMESTIC LAW

India is a common law jurisdiction with a hierarchy of courts operating in each of the country's 25 State and seven union territories. (The law discussed below extends to the entire Indian jurisdiction except the State of Kashmir and Jammu.) There is a High Court situated in every region, each having a right of appeal to the Supreme Court in New Delhi. Supreme Court precedents are binding on all courts, in all States. A decision from a High Court in one State will usually bind lower courts in other States, but this will depend on the degree of similarity between the facts of each case. Judgments from the Supreme Court and High Courts are reported in English.

Lawyers are referred to as advocates who may advise and represent the client at any level of the court hierarchy throughout India. (Supreme Court administrative procedures, eg filing and clerical work, must be undertaken by a qualified 'Advocate on Record'.) Ideally, instructions should be transferred to an advocate with expertise in child abduction matters in the State where the child is believed to be residing.

Legal aid provision is extremely limited and litigants who are not resident in India must expect to pay their own legal expenses. Legal fees vary from court to court. Supreme Court and High Court advocates normally invoice per appearance on an hourly basis and charges may be influenced by the reputation of the counsel or firm instructed.

GUARDIANSHIP AND CUSTODY

Due to the great religious diversity within India's population, family law has developed plurally, principally to accommodate India's Muslim followers who account for 11.5 per cent of the population and represent the largest of the religious minorities. Hinduism is the predominant Indian religion while the remaining population includes Sikhs, Buddhists, Christians and Parsis. Generally, children will take the religion of their father.

The foundation of India's family laws remains the Guardians and Wards Act 1890 (GAWA 1890). This enshrined the principle of guardianship and hence custodial rights. The concept of guardianship corresponds to that of parental responsibility. It has two functions: to safeguard the minor's person and property. Section 24 of GAWA 1890 defines the duties of the guardian of the person as first, custody. Other responsibilities are the minor's 'support, health and education and such other matters as the law to which the ward is subject'. Over the years, this Act has been amended with the introduction of new legislation regulating the personal laws of specific religious groups. Where these laws are silent, or do not cater for a specific faith, GAWA 1890 remains current. The sections dealing with the restoration of custody discussed above are still pertinent for Indian nationals who are non-Hindu. (The reader may be interested to note that GAWA 1890 was implemented prior to partition from Pakistan and Bangladesh and, consequently, this legislation has a continued relevance in these jurisdictions.) Regulations for the Christian and Parsi communities are not covered in this book; if further enquiry is necessary, reference should be made either to the Christian Marriage Act 1872 and the Indian Divorce Act 1889, or to the Parsi Marriage and Divorce Act 1936.

HINDU LEGISLATION

Hindu legislation applies to Hindus, Sikhs, Buddhists and Jains and their converts. Where the wife is of another faith, Hindu legislation will prevail. It also recognises adoption and accords parties the same rights as those of a natural child and parent. The Hindu Minority and Guardianship Act 1956 supplements the Guardians and Wards Act 1890. The 1956 Act confirms that minority continues until the age of 18. Responsibility for a minor's care and property is assigned to their guardian. A guardian is defined as the natural guardian or one appointed by will or the court. For legitimate offspring, the natural guardianship for minor sons and unmarried daughters rests with the father. In his absence, the mother has guardianship. For illegitimate children, the mother has the prior right of natural guardianship. In her absence, the father has the next claim. Where children are under five years of age, custody (daily care) is exercised by the mother. (The natural guardian of a married daughter under the age of 18 is her husband, the minimum marriage age for girls being 15.) The court has the authority to override legal provisions on guardianship where a party is unfit to perform this duty. Similarly, a custodian is not prevented from challenging a prior claim to guardianship where it can be shown that the child's welfare is better served by permitting custody to continue. Further provisions are outlined under 'Writ of Habeas Corpus' below.

The Hindu Marriage Act 1955 gives territorial jurisdiction to settle custody on divorce or judicial separation to a district court defined as a City Civil

Court or the Civil Court with Original Jurisdiction. Proceedings take place in camera and are heard by a judge sitting alone. The court has the discretion to make interim orders and attach conditions as it deems fit. The court should be mindful of the Hindu Minority and Guardianship Act 1956 when determining custody. However, the sole consideration is the child's interests and welfare above the legal rights of the petitioner and respondent. Hence, where a party's past conduct is a concern, it must have been of an adverse and extreme nature to merit the disqualification of their claim. A court may consider expert evidence, the wishes of elder children (although their opinions may not be given conclusive weight), the past parent–child relationship and whether the child will have the company of other children. Final orders may be subsequently varied or revoked subject to the child's interests. The 1955 Act gives a right of appeal which must be filed within 30 days of the order. Two factors determine the court with appeal jurisdiction:

(1) the rank of the judge from whom the original order was issued; and
(2) the court which usually hears appeals from the 'District Court' which is a matter of State or territorial procedure.

MUSLIM LEGISLATION

Indian Muslims, by virtue of the Muslim Personal Law (*Shari'at*) Application Act 1937, have recourse to classical Islamic principles where guardianship and custody are in question. Islam is practised throughout India with most of the Islamic schools represented. Islamic law has not, for the most part, been codified and no selection of a particular Islamic school of jurisprudence by statute or otherwise has occurred. Hence, the courts will apply legal principles determined by the sectarian belief of the parties involved. (It is advised to consider the information provided under 'Islamic Family Law' on page 12). If guardianship and/or custody is disputed, Muslim parties have recourse to remedies available under the Guardians and Wards Act 1890 and the courts will consider the child's best interests in accordance with the personal law of that child.

WRIT OF HABEAS CORPUS

India is not a signatory to the Hague Convention but under Articles 226 and 227 of the Constitution of India, a parent from whom a child has been abducted can petition one of the 'State' High Courts to issue a writ of habeas corpus against the abductor ordering the production of the minor in court. This instigates a legal mechanism, similar to the Convention, for returning an abducted child to his country of residence. First recourse should be made to this procedure. Not only is it the most correct remedy to seek where a child has been abducted into India, but it also allows the petitioner to take advantage of the relative speed and superior authority of the High Court. There is no prohibition on parents of dual nationals, or assumed dual nationals, making petitions, but the petitioner must have obtained a custody order from the appropriate foreign jurisdiction, ie the jurisdiction of residence, before making an application for a writ of habeas corpus. The existence of foreign orders, interim or final, for return or custody/ guardianship is an extremely important evidential factor and the courts in no way condone the act of abduction, particularly where it is in contempt of a foreign order or legislation.

Once filed, the court is likely to issue any necessary interim orders, directions for the surrender of the child's passport to the court or petitioner and directions for the police to investigate the child's whereabouts and delivery of the child to the court. On the parties' first appearance, interim orders may be extended pending a full hearing to determine return. For return, primary consideration is given to the child's welfare taking note of the duration of the child's presence in India which may have offered the opportunity of acclimatisation, the petitioner's ability to provide for the child and the importance of safeguarding continuity for the child. The judge may interview the child privately in chambers to determine his wishes, needs and degree of maturity. The Supreme Court has firmly expressed the view that the appropriate forum for custody resolution is within the jurisdiction 'which has the most intimate contact with issues arising in the case' (*Sandhu v Sandhu*, AIR 1984 SC 1224). Only circumstances, of which the court is satisfied beyond reasonable doubt, indicating that a return order would inflict serious harm on the child, would merit refusal of an order.

The following provisions contained in GAWA 1890 are commonly cited in support of a petition of a writ of habeas corpus (and for applications dealing with a 'domestic' abduction). Section 12 authorises the court to make an interlocutory order to produce a minor at a certain time and place and make any temporary custody and protection orders as it thinks fit pending a full hearing. Section 25 stipulates that, where a minor is removed from the custody of his guardian, the court may order the child's return if it is satisfied that it is in the child's welfare to do so. Section 25(5) allows for such an order to be made in favour of a guardian who is resident outside the jurisdiction or for the appointment of guardian who is resident outside the jurisdiction. Section 26 stipulates that a court-appointed guardian may not remove the child from the area of the court's jurisdiction without leave. Consent may be given in general or specific terms. In the event of two sets of litigation occurring, the High Court takes jurisdiction.

International child abduction law in India stands substantially modified in terms of a very recent Supreme Court judgment in the matter of *Dhanwanti Joshi v Madhay Unde*, reported as JT 1997 (8) SC 720, handed down on 4 November 1997. It deals with the provisions and case-law analysis relating to the Hindu Minority and Guardianship Act 1980, read with the GAWA 1890. These two enactments principally govern the law relating to child custody under Indian law.

Under Indian law, ie the GAWA 1890 and the Hindu Minority and Guardianship Act 1956, the prime consideration is the welfare of the child, although s 6(a) of the latter Act says that the custody of a minor who has not yet attained the age of five shall ordinarily be left with the mother.

It was held in para 31 of the judgment:

> 'So far as non-Convention countries are concerned, or where the removal related to a period before adopting the Convention, the law is that the court to which the child is removed will consider the question on merits bearing the welfare of the child as of paramount importance and consider the order of the foreign court as only a factor to be taken into consideration as stated in *McKee v McKee* [1951] AC 352, unless the court think it fit to exercise summary jurisdiction in the interests of the child and its prompt return is for its welfare, as explained in *Re L* [1974] 1 All ER 913 (CA). As recently as 1996–1997, it has been held in *Re P (A Minor) (Child Abduction: Non-Convention Country)* (1996) 3 FCR 233 (CA) by Ward LJ (*Current Law Year Book*, pp 165–166) that in deciding whether to order the return of a child who has been abducted from his or her country of habitual residence – which was not a party to the Hague Convention 1980 – the courts' overriding consideration must be the child's welfare. There is no need for the judge to attempt to apply the provisions of Article 13 of the Convention by ordering the child's return unless a grave risk of harm was established.'

From the above mandate of law, it is clear that the courts in India now would not exercise a summary jurisdiction to return children to the foreign country of habitual residence.

It has also been held in para 31 of the judgment that orders relating to the custody of children are, by their very nature, not final, but are interlocutory in nature and subject to modification at any future time upon proof of change of circumstances requiring change of custody, but such change in custody must be proved to be in the paramount interests of the child. This was the position of law laid down by the Supreme Court of India in *Rosy Jacob v Jacob A Chakramakkai* [1973] (1) SCC 840, explicitly reiterated in the above-mentioned 1997 ruling.

Before this ruling was handed down, there was case-law to the contrary, allowing enforcement of foreign court custody orders on the principle of comity on a case-to-case basis. Such orders were normally enforced by initiating habeas corpus petitions in the High Court where the child was situated, or directly in the Supreme Court of India under Article 32 of the Constitution of India.

It is pertinent to mention that the custody order of a foreign court is only one of the factors which will be taken into consideration by a court of law in India, which will instead form an independent judgment on the merits of the matter with regard to the welfare of the children. Lastly, superior financial capacity cannot be a sole ground for disturbing the children from their mother's custody.

FOREIGN ORDERS

Sections 13 and 14 of the Code of Civil Procedure obliges the courts to give conclusive weight to foreign judgments relating to the same matter being adjudicated on the following conditions:

- the originating court had jurisdiction;
- the merits of the case were considered and rights of natural justice were preserved;
- international law was correctly applied; and
- the order was not contrary to Indian law.

PASSPORTS

A separate application for surrender of a passport to prevent a child's removal from the jurisdiction can be lodged during the course of custody proceedings.

CONTACTS

Ministry of Law, Justice and Commercial Affairs
Shastri Bhavan
Ragendra Prasad Road
New Delhi-11011

Iran

- *CONVENTIONS*
  None

DOMESTIC LAW

The system is based on Islam (see Part 1). Iran is regarded as the heart of Shi'ite Islamic worship. The official doctrine of Iran are those principles formulated by the Inthna-Asharia school, the largest of the Shia Muslim sects. Children of Iranian fathers will take their father's nationality. Consequently, guardianship decisions will be taken by the Sharia courts according to Islamic principles. Legal practitioners are able to advise and provide representation at all level of courts throughout the country.

CUSTODY

A mother has the prior claim to custody until a boy is weaned at two years and a girl attains her seventh year. A non-Muslim mother will be disqualified from her custodial claim to a Muslim child. The father has the next claim; thereafter paternal relatives are favoured over maternal relatives. Remarriage, whether to a relative or stranger, will cause the mother's right of custody to cease. It is recoverable if the subsequent marriage ends.

A custodial mother will be expected to reside in a place sufficiently near the father to permit access and the exercise of supervision and other forms of guardianship. Relocation to a more distant location or travel abroad with the child will require paternal consent. Fathers also require the custodial mother's permission to travel unless the child's interests dictate to the contrary or the mother has temporarily lost custody because of remarriage.

ACCESS

Non-custodial parents are entitled to access, usually on a weekly basis. The custodian is not obliged to allow access at home, but is expected co-operate with arrangements for visits elsewhere.

CONVENTION LAW AND PROCEDURE

Iran is a non-Convention country.

CONTACTS

Ministry of Justice
Pan Zadeh Khordad
Tehran
Iran
Tel: (00) 98 21 3221
Fax: (00) 98 21 3027

Iraq

- *CONVENTIONS*
  None

DOMESTIC LAW

The system is based on Islam (see Part 1).

The Iraqi Civil Code, Article 17, confirms that when issues of guardianship arise the national law of the minor is applicable. Children take their father's nationality, hence Iraqi law will prevail. Advice and legal representation is provided by attorneys able to appear in Civil and Sharia courts. Decisions on personal status are taken by the Sharia courts which have exclusive jurisdiction (other religious faiths having their own religious courts). Iraqi law is founded on Islamic jurisprudence. Modern legislation is codified and supported by case-law. Where statutory guidance is not available, the court will consider principles of Sharia law.

CUSTODY

According to Article 57, Act No 188/1959 amended by Act No 21/1978, the mother has the first claim for custody during marriage and thereafter, unless this is deemed detrimental to the minor. The father has the next claim. If both parents are unable or deemed unsuitable to have a custody, a third party will be appointed with consideration being given to the child's interests. In the event that the mother has custody and the father is dead or unsuitable, any of the child's relatives may challenge the mother's right to custody until the child becomes an adult. A mother will lose custody should she subsequently marry a man who is not related to the minor within a prohibited degree.

DURATION OF CUSTODY

Article 57 stipulates that guardianship of infancy terminates when a child reaches his or her tenth year. The custodial period may be extended, by order of the court, until the child completes his or her fifteenth year. Such a decision will be made in the child's interests and medical reports and those of local committees can be submitted for the court's consideration. Throughout this time, the father will continue to play a supervisory role. At 16 years, a minor has the choice of which relative he or she wishes to reside with until reaching the age of 18. This must have court approval.

TRAVEL ADVICE

At the present time, the Foreign and Commonwealth Office strongly advise British nationals not to attempt visiting Iraq. There is no representation for British nationals within Iraq. Responsibility for matters involving Iraq are handled by the British Embassy in Jordan. International communication remains difficult.

CONVENTION LAW AND PROCEDURE

Iraq is a non-Convention country.

CONTACTS

Ministry of Justice
Baghdad
Iraq

Foreign nationals are advised to make all official enquiries through their national embassy.

Ireland

■ *CONVENTIONS*

Hague — Effective date: 1 October 1991
European — Effective date: 1 October 1991

DOMESTIC LAW

Ireland operates a unified common law system. Family law sources are to be found in legislation, the main statute referring to custody being the Guardianship of Infants Act 1964 (GIA 1964) as amended by the Status of Children Act 1986. Judicial decisions are reported in the *Irish Law Reports*, *Irish Law Reports Monthly*, *Family Law Journal* and the *Irish Law Times Reports*. The legal profession has two branches: solicitors and barristers, the majority of whom will have a specialist area of practice. Although, both share rights of audience up to the High Court, solicitors seldom represent a client at this level. When bringing Irish proceedings, instructions must be transferred to a solicitor.

All family hearings take place in camera. This is a rule that is strictly adhered to. The courts will take a negative view of media and press coverage. Under no circumstances should any family proceedings held in camera receive any publicity whatsoever or wheresoever.

There is no specialist family court and the court of first instance will depend on the nature of the case. Judges may vary from day to day but they will usually have expertise in family proceedings. Outside Dublin, the district and circuit courts set aside specific days for family hearings. Generally, hearings for custody or access take place in the district court with a right of appeal to the circuit court. The circuit courts have original jurisdiction for divorce and judicial separation and they are required, prior to the issue of a decree, to be satisfied that the appropriate arrangements for the child's care have been made for a child of the marriage. Right of appeal (by way of a rehearing) lies to the High Court, but not for appeal decisions from the District Court. The High Court remains the appropriate forum to handle more difficult cases and these may involve issues of abduction and prevention. A right of appeal exists from the High Court to the Supreme Court on points of law only.

CUSTODY

The principle of parental responsibility, termed guardianship, is incorporated into the Irish Constitution under Article 42.1 which requires 'parents to provide according to their means, for the religious and moral, intellectual, physical and social education of their children' and echoed by GIA 1964. However, this joint obligation is restricted to parents of legitimate children. Guardianship will be exercised by an unmarried mother alone unless the father has applied under GIA 1964 for a joint guardianship, custody or access order. Once an unmarried father has been appointed a guardian, he acquires rights of custody and access which can be enforced by the courts. Cohabitation or a simple agreement will not be sufficient to establish shared rights. Unmarried couples must formalise guardianship by court order even when they are in accord. Alternatively, a natural father may pursue the adoption of his own child.

Until recently, divorce was not available under Irish law, making judicial separation the most favoured remedy for separating couples. It is expected that divorce will become the preferred remedy for couples who have lived apart for four years or more. While annulment permits remarriage, its application is minimal causing judicial separation to be the most favoured remedy. Grounds for judicial separation are similar to those for divorce in other jurisdictions. Terms of custody may be privately agreed. However, the courts have a duty to examine and approve arrangements for children up to the age of 18 and, if necessary to amend them if they could adversely affect the child's welfare. Separated or unmarried parents can also make applications for custodial orders to any of 23 district courts. Interim orders will be granted if matters affecting the child can be shown to be of an immediate and urgent nature.

Under s 3 of GIA 1964, any court deliberating custody or guardianship 'shall regard the welfare of the infant as the first and paramount consideration'. Proceedings are traditionally adversarial but, where possible, mediation and/or informal resolution is encouraged. The court has the authority to appoint independent experts to report on and consider the child's wishes. The judge will either interview the child in chambers or ask the expert to do so. Joint custody is unlikely. Orders will divide parental rights into custody and access, and may contain precise directions for access detailing arrangements for supervision, holidays, frequency of contact, foreign travel and passports. Without a court order prohibiting removal or restricting custody, there is presumption that a parent of a child has consent to take the child abroad without the consent of the other parent regardless of marital status. If consent is not forthcoming, formal leave from the court permitting removal should be sought from the district court. An unmarried mother has the right to remove the child from Ireland if she is the child's sole guardian. Variation or discharge may occur in the future if the child's circumstances have altered sufficiently to make the enforcement of existing orders contrary to the child's welfare.

WARDSHIP

Wardship causes all matters affecting the child's upbringing to become the court's responsibility. Decisions such as education, holidays, maintenance, etc will rest with the court. It is possible to ward a child under the age of 18 through an application to either the circuit court or High Court. Any person having an interest, for example the guardian, a natural father or local authority may apply. This said, wardship applications are comparatively rare and are resorted to, if at all, in circumstances where it is thought desirable to have independent protection of the minor's property interests. Where a minor has no property interests, wardship may be decreed if this is thought to be in the minor's best interest. The court is empowered to grant the necessary orders to restrict removal, to facilitate any search for a child and safeguard the child's safe return out of the jurisdiction. Parties who refuse to comply with terms of wardship will be held in contempt of court, punishable by unlimited imprisonment. This remedy could assist in the resolution of complex disputes where the Convention process is exhausted or not available.

PASSPORTS

A parent may carry their child's details on their passport or apply for a separate passport only with the written consent of the other parent. If the other parent is dead, this must be proved by producing a death certificate. If the other guardian unreasonably refuses consent or cannot be located, an application to the court may be made to dispense with the other guardian's consent. An illegitimate child will automatically be placed on his or her mother's passport and a their mother must give consent for a separate child's passport to be issued. GIA 1964 should be used to apply for the surrender of passports carrying a child's details. A guardian may subsequently withdraw consent and may apply, even where consent is not formally withdrawn, for an order prohibiting the child's removal from the jurisdiction.

EXIT BAN

There is no presumption that one joint guardian has the consent of the other to remove the child from the jurisdiction. There is no formal procedure. However, making an ex parte application under s 11 of GIA 1964 to the circuit court or High Court is an effective means of alerting the police, emigration, airport and port authorities. Applications will be given speedy attention and should stipulate that the order is to prevent a named child's removal from the jurisdiction without the consent of the other parent, seek the surrender of passports and request a further order for the solicitor to telephone the police (*Gardai*) to inform and alert emigration and all points of departure from Ireland. It should also require the abducting parent to produce the child in court within a certain period. In practice, the High Court will grant orders on hearing oral evidence from the applicant parent. If the police and other authorities are on notice of an order prohibiting removal, they may notify the applicant parent that they are aware that the child may be about to be removed from the jurisdiction. If the other guardian breaches the order, it is for the applicant parent to apply again for an order holding the other guardian in contempt.

FOREIGN ORDERS AND PROCEEDINGS

The rules for the recognition of foreign divorce are complex. In simple terms, the Irish courts will recognise and respect such a decree if either spouse was domiciled in the jurisdiction in which the divorce was granted on the date proceedings began. (Refer to the Domicile and Recognition of Foreign Divorces Act 1986.) This recognition will permit remarriage and the Irish courts will also entertain applications in relation to maintenance if circumstances have changed since the making of the foreign divorce decree.

Beyond the terms of the Conventions, there is no precedent or policy establishing the comity principle. Consequently the courts are unlikely to stay Irish proceedings.

CRIMINAL REMEDY

Abduction remedies exist but do not encompass acts of parental abduction, although an abductor and/or third party assisting them who refuses to comply with a civil order will be guilty of contempt of court. Kidnapping and false imprisonment are offences at common law. Foreign warrants will not be carried out. However, this will not disqualify a left parent from exploiting civil remedies under the Conventions or warding the child, nor will it prevent the instigation of police procedures. Both Conventions are incorporated into Irish legislation via the Child Abduction and Enforcement of Custody Orders Act 1991. The Central Authority will verify applications to ensure Convention criteria are met and that any attached documentation is correct. Once accepted, the case will be forwarded to a solicitor who will be one of a list of solicitors, known to have experience in Convention applications, compiled by the Central Authority. As all return applications are legally aided and must be filed at the High Court sitting in Dublin, the applicant's representative will be a legal aid lawyer based in Dublin. The Central Authority will notify the police of the application and request that they trace or verify the child's whereabouts. This process occurs within 24 hours of the application's receipt.

Application proceedings are begun by summons requesting the child's return and ex parte orders will be made even if the child has not been located. Service will depend on when the whereabouts of the respondent are determined. Ex parte orders will cater for care arrangements to safeguard the child's welfare pending a full hearing, prohibit removal from the jurisdiction. Furthermore, s 36 of the 1991 Act authorises the High Court to order disclosure of the child's whereabouts from any person believed to have relevant information. The ex parte order is usually made returnable on the same date set for the hearing of an interlocutory Notice of Motion seeking the same reliefs. Where appropriate, the Notice of Motion is disposed of by way of an undertaking by the respondent agreeing not to remove the child from the jurisdiction pending the hearing of the application.

The summons will order the parties to a hearing before the Master of the High Court and give the respondent the option of returning the child within a stipulated period (about a week) or attending court to file an appearance and defence. If service has not occurred by the return date, the Master may grant a new date and extend time to file a defence. Once a defence has been filed, the Master will transfer papers to the High Court for a hearing. In child abduction matters, it is accepted that an early hearing is of the essence and, as a departure from usual practice, the High Court will fix a date for the hearing prior to receiving the papers from the Master. The hearing in the High Court is before a single judge and evidence is given on affidavit from parties and expert witnesses. The court may consent to parties to submit oral evidence.

The courts have not defined 'habitual residence' as this is regarded as a mixed issue of law and fact. For the same reason, the courts have not defined what constitutes a defence under either Convention. However, the Supreme Court has held that the burden of proof establishing such a defence should be higher than that required for a civil case, ie the balance of probabilities but less than required for criminal liability ie beyond reasonable doubt. If it has not been possible to observe the prescribed time-limit of 12 months under Article 12, because the child's whereabouts were concealed, the applicant parent will not be barred from bringing an action, provided he has acted promptly once the child's location was known. Nevertheless, a long delay may support grounds for raising a defence.

Conditions may be attached to an order directing the child's return. Return orders are enforceable unless the order stipulates it should not operate until an appeal is heard. Filing an appeal is not an automatic stay on enforcement. However, in practice, it is accepted that once an appeal is filed the order shall not be acted on. Nevertheless, a successful applicant remains free to enforce the order and an appellant may apply separately to the Appeal Court forthwith for a stay. Right of appeal is to the Supreme Court, sitting in

PART

2

Dublin, on points of law. The Supreme Court also attaches importance to hearing appeals on child abduction as quickly as possible. Only where there is clear evidence indicating that a trial judge's findings are wholly inconsistent with the evidence before the Supreme Court, will an appeal on a finding of fact go ahead as the Supreme Court considers itself bound by the findings of fact by the High Court.

COSTS AND LEGAL AID

All return applicants qualify for legal aid. To take advantage of this provision, instructions must be transferred to a legal aid solicitor employed by a Law Centre. Legal aid is administered by the Legal Aid Board which operates a network of Centres located in Ireland's cities and major towns. It is not always possible to comply with a parent's request for a particular solicitor. However, the degree of available expertise in family law will be high as this area of law represents 90 per cent of the legal aid case-load. Contact applications will be subject to a means test of disposable income and capital. The current levels for eligibility are £4,000 and £20,000 respectively. Ireland is also a party to the European Agreement for the Transmission of Applications 1977 (see p 11). Legal aid is available on an emergency basis and there is an appeals procedure for refusals.

CONTACTS

CENTRAL AUTHORITY

Department of Equality and Law Reform
43/49 Mespil Road
Dublin 4
Tel: (353) 1 667 0344
Fax: (353) 1 667 0367

OTHER AGENCIES

Irish Association of Family Lawyers
Law Library
Four Courts
Dublin 7

The Legal Aid Board
Head Office
St Stephen's Green House
Earlsfort Terrace
Dublin 2

Gardai
Crime Branch
Phoenix Park
Dublin 8
Tel: (353) 1 677 1156

The Incorporated Law Society
Blackhall Place
Dublin 7
Tel: (353) 1 671 0711
Fax: (353) 1 671 0704

PART

2

Israel

■ *CONVENTION*
Hague – Effective date: 1 December 1991

DOMESTIC LAW

The Israeli legal system is based on common and civil law. There is a single legal profession whose members are referred to as attorneys. They are able to advise the client and represent them in court on receipt of transferred instructions. 1995 saw the introduction of a family court system with specific jurisdiction for family cases and, therefore, for custodial disputes (see p 128).

RELIGIOUS COURTS

Being a religious State, Israel has a system of religious courts to accommodate the different faiths of its population with authority to decide cases involving family law and personal status issues. The Rabbinical court has jurisdiction for Jewish citizens, the Sharia court for Muslims and others for Christians. This dual system will be significant only for parties who are Israeli citizens and who are married at the time of an abduction. There is a concurrent jurisdiction between the religious and civil courts. Neither court is superior, their status being parallel. Should a religious court exceed its authority, final ruling rests with the Supreme Court.

The Rabbinical courts have sole jurisdiction for divorce. However, custody may be determined by the civil court even while a divorce is pending. Sharia courts have exclusive jurisdiction on custody during divorce proceedings. Although Convention applications will at all times be heard in a civil court, a legal stalemate may arise should the abducting parent obtain a 'no exit order' from the Rabbinical court to prevent a child's removal, thus contradicting any return order issued by the civil court. It may also cause the left parent unwittingly to 'acquiesce' by defending Rabbinical court proceedings. The Supreme Court has not yet had the opportunity to rule on this issue. Should these circumstances arise, an applicant would be entitled to ask the Supreme Court to cancel the no exit order. It is expected that a request of this nature would be successful.

CUSTODY

Under s 15 of the Capacity and Guardianship Act 1962, married couples hold parental rights termed 'the guardianship of parents' jointly; the provision expressly states that this includes the right to determine the child's place of residence. Section 17 of the Act states that it is the duty of parents to act in the interests of their child. As discussed above, custody may be considered in the religious or civil courts with family jurisdiction.

In Israeli law, precedent has established the rule that where a child's welfare is a serious consideration, it should be the court's sole consideration, overriding other considerations. In custody proceedings, the consideration of the child's best interests is always paramount. The courts have been advised to approach such decisions with the aim of finding the least detrimental alternative. There is no statutory welfare criteria, but existing case-law indicates that the physical, mental and emotional well-being of children are primary factors and great importance is placed on the maintenance of continuity and emotional ties. Precedent also indicates a reluctance to part siblings and mothers from extremely young children. Religious courts will adhere to the principle with regard to the child's best interest. However, its implementation will be according to the principles of the religion in question which may differ from those followed in civil law.

The 1962 Act allows civil or family courts to take account of the child's wishes which may be expressed within a welfare officer's report, if ordered, but may 'not be accorded decisive, determinative weight'. Both civil and religious courts will accept evidence from an expert psychologist, usually via a report and, in the majority of cases, regardless of the children's ages, a welfare report will be requested.

NO EXIT ORDERS

These orders, sometimes referred to as 'stop' orders, can be issued against an abductor and/or a child to prevent their departure from the jurisdiction. Such orders will be issued on an ex parte basis on the day of filing by the court with family jurisdiction, or Rabbinical courts. They are served on the national police headquarters which notifies all terminals of exit from the country.

PASSPORTS

Passports for Israeli minors must be authorised by both parents. Parents can no longer register their children on their own passports. An order can be made to surrender passports to the court or to an attorney.

WRIT OF HABEAS CORPUS

The High Court of Justice has the power to issue this writ. The abductor has the burden of proving that real harm will be caused by returning the child to the other parent. Unfortunately, this remedy is seldom effective and is used only when a non-Convention country is involved.

CRIMINAL REMEDY

It is an offence to remove a child from his legal guardian, but such charges are not known to have been applied against a parent.

CONVENTION LAW AND PROCEDURE

The Hague Convention is incorporated into Israeli law (by number 13555 of the Reshumot of the Knesset). Prior to acceptance, the Central Authority will check that an application satisfies Convention criteria and that the relevant documents are attached. Regulations stipulate that applications and documentation be submitted in Hebrew. However, the majority of the judiciary are fluent in English, hence there is a de facto acceptance of applications made in English. There is no formal procedure for the Central Authority to attempt to negotiate a voluntary return and it will rarely get involved in this process. The Central Authority cannot transfer instructions to a lawyer on the applicant's behalf but it will provide a list of about 20 attorneys whose specialist expertise in child abduction/Convention cases is confirmed. Legally aided clients will be appointed a lawyer who is employed by the legal aid board. Although the Central Authority's direct involvement ceases from this point, it retains a coordinating role in relation to issues such as contact, voluntary settlement and liaison with Interpol. When the child's whereabouts are unknown, the best advice is to obtain a court order for police assistance, although the Central Authority can secure police assistance directly.

Once instructions are confirmed, the appointed attorney will lodge a petition with the court. The Family Court Act 1995 has transferred jurisdiction for family cases from the five district courts to five specialist family courts sitting in the major Israeli centres. The practical change-over is not yet complete and, so far, two family courts are operating. Cases in other regional jurisdictions are brought before one of three district courts which continue to have family jurisdiction. The petition will make a request for return and seek any necessary interim or protective orders. It will be served on the respondent who will be ordered to file a written defence no later than two days prior to the hearing. According to Israeli regulations, a hearing must take place within 15 days of filing. Proceedings are adversarial and are not held in camera unless a specific request is made. A petitioner's attendance at the hearing is strongly recommended. It improves the applicant's chances of success and overcomes the problem of placing the child in the temporary care of a third party. If the petition is defended, the court has the discretion to determine a schedule and the procedure to be followed, being mindful of the respondent's right to have adequate time to prepare a defence and the summary nature of Convention proceedings. Judgment must be rendered within six weeks of filing.

The case will be heard by a judge sitting alone. Parties can submit expert psychologist evidence, usually by report, and the court will take account of the objections of children depending on the degree of maturity or under-standing. Either party has the option to request a social worker's report and the court also has the authority to initiate one. A petitioner is entitled to object to a report. The report is prepared by a regional welfare officer who will be a professional social worker. The child's opinions will be recorded within the report which will contain an evaluation of the child's environment and emotional state, regardless of age, and the likely effect that a return to the place of habitual residence could have on a child.

HABITUAL RESIDENCE

Precedent has established that Israeli citizenship or cultural and family links are not determinative factors for habitual residence. However, the regular place of residence indicated by the child's physical presence over a relatively short period of time is a determinative factor. A couple's shared intent to relocate or return to Israel, followed by a child's unilateral removal to Israel, is not deemed sufficient consent to alter the child's habitual residence.

DEFENCES

ARTICLE 13(a)

Consent must equate to a clear agreement to the child's removal or retention. Acquiescence does not require a specific awareness of the Convention, merely a general understanding that removal was in derogation of the petitioner's rights. Should an abductor begin custody proceedings prior to or during a Convention application, the participation in this litigation by the parent seeking return may be held to be an acceptance of Israel's jurisdiction and therefore acquiescence. Consequently, a custody petition brought by the parent seeking return will be regarded in the same way.

ARTICLE 13(b)

There is a very high threshold for defences under this sub-Article, and an 'intolerable situation' is interpreted as involving a similarly extreme position for the child, as does the 'grave risk' of physical or psychological harm. A child fearful of return due to the 'demonising' of the left parent by the abductor and/or the refusal of the primary carer to accompany return, are examples of unsuccessful defences. Allegations of adverse circumstances must therefore be shown to be of an extreme nature and based on fact.

ARTICLE 13(c)

There is no specific age limit for a child to be deemed to possess sufficient maturity and understanding to express his objections. Objections put forward must be based on fact, as opposed to fears resulting from the influence of an abductor or third party.

APPEALS

A party has seven days from the date of judgment to file an appeal. Appeals on decision from the family court are considered by the district court. There is a further right of appeal to the Supreme Court in Jerusalem with leave of the district court. Should an order come from the district court, an appeal may be made to the Supreme Court. It is possible for an appeal to delay the enforcement of an order where the court has specifically granted a stay of execution. In principle, the appeal hearing should occur within 30 days of filing the appeal. In reality, it is common for this procedure to take several months.

COSTS AND LEGAL AID

A client instructing an attorney privately is free to negotiate fees. Most attorneys will charge a flat fee for Hague cases. Experienced attorneys will usually charge $10,000, exclusive of taxation at 17 per cent, or more to handle the case in the court of first instance. Appeals are billed separately. There are no costs for filing. However, other disbursements for administration, telephone and fax expenses, etc are also charged separately.

Israel has made a reservation on Article 26. However, legal aid is provided to those applicants who would qualify in their own jurisdiction. Requests accompanied by official letters and documentation proving entitlement should be sent to the Central Authority where they it will be assessed by a private council. This process can take up to three months. Eligible applicants will be allocated a lawyer employed by the legal aid body but note, although the lawyer may be an experienced family law attorney, there is no guarantee he will be familiar with the Convention.

CONTACTS

CENTRAL AUTHORITY

The Attorney General
International Department
Ministry of Justice
PO Box 1087
Jerusalem 91010
Israel
Tel: 972 (2) 670 8797
Fax: 972 (2) 628 7668

OTHER AGENCIES

(Children's Rights Organisation)
National Council for the Welfare of Children
19 Teverya Street
Jerusalem
Tel: 972 (2) 625 6102

Italy

■ *CONVENTIONS*

Hague – Effective date: 1 May 1995
European – Effective date: 1 June 1995

DOMESTIC LAW

The principles of Italian family law are found in Articles 79 to 455 of the first book of the Civil Code (*Codice Civile*). Unlike common law systems, precedent is not deemed a source of law. However, it is customary for judgments and interpretations widely adopted by judges and Court of Cassation rulings to be followed.

Lawyers are termed *avvocato* or *procuratore*, the latter having less than six years' experience. Some lawyers specialise in family cases; very few specialise in abduction. Any person, regardless of nationality or Italian residence, may instigate a civil action. On divorce, custody issues are settled in the local civil courts (*Tribunale*). Disputes over custody and parental authority are heard in the Juvenile Court (*Tribunale dei Minori*). Appeals from both courts will be heard in the Court of Appeal (*Corte d'Apello*). Children's hearing are not open to the public.

CUSTODY (*AFFIDAMENTO*)

On divorce or separation, custody is settled simultaneously in the civil courts. Parental authority and custody cases after divorce or separation are heard by the Tutelary judge sitting in the juvenile court.

MARRIED PARENTS

Married parents automatically hold, jointly, parental authority (*potesta dei genitori*) which must be exercised by mutual agreement. Consequently, removal of children, where the parents remain married, and no court orders are in place, is wrongful unless it is by mutual agreement.

SEPARATED OR DIVORCED PARENTS

In cases of separation or divorce, the issue of custody is regulated by the separation or divorce decree.

There are two possibilities (pursuant to Article 155 of the Civil Code). Either one parent is given the right unilaterally to determine the place of residence of a child, or the right is shared or restricted pursuant to orders of the court.

UNMARRIED PARENTS

Unmarried parents who live together are in the same position as married parents (pursuant to Article 317 bis of the Civil Code). Where unmarried parents do not live together, and object to the acquisition of parental authority by recognition or judicial declaration, custody rights (including the right to change place of residence) belong to the parent with whom the child lives.

GENERAL AUTHORS' NOTE

This view of this aspect of Italian law has not, at least in the English jurisdiction, been accepted as necessarily definitive. There are arguments to the effect that unmarried fathers who have recognised their children but who do not live with them may have a joint right to determine the child's place of residence.

WELFARE

The paramountcy of a child's moral and material interest is the fundamental principle applied to all hearings relating to children. Parents' wishes and those of children sufficiently mature enough to express them (usually 14 or over) will be considered. Evidence from expert witnesses is admitted.

ENFORCEMENT

In order to obtain enforcement of an Italian custody order, Italian courts generally rely as much as possible on the cooperation and advice of the social services (*assistenti sociali*), although the actual decisions are taken by the court. Foreign court orders are automatically effective on condition they do not contravene Italian public policy and that the defendant's rights have been observed.

ORDER TO RETURN

Where a wrongful abduction into Italy has occurred and neither Convention is applicable, a foreign return order issued in the requesting country may be recognised and enforced, if a reciprocal Convention is in place.

PASSPORTS

Parents who have rights of custody must give their permission before a child can be issued with a passport. When parents are separated, authority for issuance must be obtained from the Tutelary judge. An order for the surrender of a parent's and/or a child's current passport can be obtained provided substantial grounds are established to demonstrate the imminent danger of the child's removal by a parent from Italy.

FRONTIER CHECKS

A court order is required and must be registered with the frontier police. An order for the surrender of passports would be adequate for this purpose. A parent travelling with minors will usually be stopped at the frontier.

CRIMINAL REMEDY

Under Articles 573 and 574 of the Penal Code, it is an offence for any person to take or detain a child under the age of 18 thereby removing the child from the lawful control of any person or institution with custody rights. A parent who shares parental authority can be indicted for the crime of child abduction.

CONVENTION LAW AND PROCEDURE

Italy is a relatively new signatory and consequently the smooth integration of Hague procedures into the legal system has yet to be completed. Requesting parents may need to pursue constant communication with all the government offices and services involved throughout to ensure their file is processed, particularly if the child's whereabouts are unknown and/or the child is at risk.

The appointed Central Authority is the Department of Juvenile Justice. Applications are accepted from a petitioner personally or via the relevant Central Authority. Assessment is made by one of three judges who staff the Central Authority to ensure Convention criteria are satisfied. At present, this procedure takes between one week and 10 days. However, the judge will communicate directly with the applicant should further information or documentation be required. To avoid delay, it is strongly advised to provide Italian translations and to attach a declaration from the requesting Central Authority stating that the child has been wrongfully removed or retained. The provision of as much translated support documentation as possible will prevent further delays at later stages of the procedure. The Central Authority is empowered to call upon a special division of the police, referred to as the Minors Division, for assistance and in certain circumstances the help of 'any qualified governmental administrative body'. The authority is not permitted to seek out the services of private lawyers and enquiry agents nor can it refer applicants to Italian lawyers specialising in abduction and related cases, although those parents who wish to may do so themselves.

Applications are forwarded from the Central Authority to the Public Prosecutor of the juvenile court in one of 26 regional jurisdictions, the appropriate region being where the child is known or presumed to be living. If the police have failed to locate the child and no other evidence is available, applications can be sent to the juvenile court in Rome. Applications are transferable on the discovery of a child's whereabouts. Applications sent direct to the juvenile court will be accepted although filing and stamping fees will be incurred and the Public Prosecutor is also mandatorily required to intervene during these proceedings. Bypassing the Central Authority is recommended only in urgent cases and when an experienced attorney has been appointed.

The application to the juvenile court will seek an interlocutory order for the return of the child to his or her country of habitual residence. Once filed, a hearing date will be set and the Central Authority will be notified which, in turn, will inform the applicant. The case will be heard by three tribunal judges who are mandatorily required to interview people living with the child. However, there is no statutory duty to question the left-behind parent who is not required to attend. Questioning of a child is at the court's discretion. However, it is unlikely for children below the age of 12 to 14 to be interviewed. Applications under the European Convention will follow the same route except for the hearing. The juvenile court usually issues an enforcement decree in chambers and parties will be heard only where clarification or additional documentation is required.

A decision ought to be forthcoming from the court 30 days from the date of filing the application. In reality, due to pressure on court schedules, orders are likely to be issued approximately 40 to 60 days after filing. Decisions are instantly effective and there is a right of appeal to the Court of Cassation. Appeals to the Court of Cassation may be made on points of law only. The appeal procedure can take as long as two years; the order will continue to remain enforceable during this period.

In the event that an abductor refuses to comply with the order, it becomes the duty of the Chief Public Prosecutor, in the region of the child's residence, to ask the police Minors Division for assistance in removing the child, usually with the support of social services.

COSTS AND LEGAL AID

There is no automatic right to legal aid. It is only granted to individuals who are able to prove they have minimal income and are resident in Italy. The creation of additional legal aid resources in not envisaged for the future. Lawyers' fees and disbursements will vary according to the complexity of the case. Expect extra costs for translation and enforcement orders, but charges for filing and stamping in Convention applications are not levied. Fees are negotiable between lawyer and client. Due to the time-consuming nature of abduction cases, parents are advised to agree on a fixed fee rather than an hourly rate.

CONTACTS

CENTRAL AUTHORITY

Ministero di Grazia e Giustizia
Ufficio Centrale per la Giustizia Minorile
Via Giulia 131
00186 Rome
Italy
Tel: 39(6) 6880 7139
Fax: 39(6) 6880 7087

OTHER AGENCIES

'*Associazione per i diritti del fanciullo*' (Association for Children's Rights) deals specifically with the issue of abduction providing information and support.

ANAI (National Association for Children) is involved with wider issues relating to children. Abduction represents part of this organisation's work.

(National Association for Children)
ANAI
Via Kerbaker N 86
0123 Napoli
Contact: Rita Chiliberti, President
Tel: 3981 558 5579

(Ministry of Justice)
Ministero di Grazia e Giustizia
Via Aurenula 70
00186 Roma

(Association for Children's Rights)
Associazione per i diritti del fanciullo
Via Montalto Vecchio N 301
41055 Montalto
Contact: Bruno Poli, President
Tel/Fax: 59 386 654

(Rome Lawyers Association)
Consiglio dell'Ordine degli Avvocati e Procurati di Roma
Palazzo di Giustizia
Piazza Cavour
00193 Roma
Tel: 6 687 5294; 6 687 5296

Servizio Sociale Internazionale
Sezione per l'Italia
96 Via V Veneto
88187 Roma
Contact: Alessandro Ciuffa, Director

PART

2

Libya

- *CONVENTIONS*
  None

DOMESTIC LAW

The system is based on Islam (see Part 1). The Libyan population are followers of the Maliki doctrine and personal status laws have developed from this tradition. In 1981, private legal practice was abolished. All lawyers are now State employees of the People's Legal Practice Department of the Ministry of Justice. Free legal advice is available from government-run law offices. Foreign nationals may use this service but must pay for any legal representation. Charges can be negotiated. Current legislation is founded in the Family Law 1954.

Article 16 of the Civil Code confirms that the national law of the minor will determine the applicable national law on issues of guardianship. Children take their nationality from their father. Consequently, Libyan law will prevail when questions of guardianship are in dispute. In principle, the mother is acknowledged as the most appropriate party to perform the duties of custodian. It is possible for a non-Muslim mother to be appointed custodian. However, she is more likely to be given access. Foreign parents are not prevented from applying for custody or access. If they are successful, their rights must be exercised within the Libyan jurisdiction. Should a custodial mother remarry she will forfeit her right to custody irrevocably.

Proof of a father's consent is a prerequisite for any child leaving the country. Children travelling with non-Libyan mothers must travel on separate passports. There are no restrictions placed on fathers travelling with their children.

ACCESS

Libya recognises the non-custodial parent's right to access and the child's right to see that parent.

CONVENTION LAW AND PROCEDURE

Libya is a non-Convention country.

CONTACTS

There is an organisation called the Higher Committee for Children. *reunite* can give advice as to how to contact this organisation.

Morocco

- *CONVENTIONS*
  None

DOMESTIC LAW

The system is based on Islam (see Part 1). The greater part of the population is Muslim, they have recourse to the Code of Personal Status and Succession 1958 (referred to as the *Mudawana*), provisions on custody are contained within Book III, Articles 97 to 111. Non Jewish and Muslim foreigners are also subject to this law. Morocco continues to apply Maliki principles when determining issues of personal status. This area of law has developed with virtually no influence from other doctrines. Personal status legislation has developed plurally to accommodate Morocco's Jewish minority. Hebraic law covers both Moroccan and foreign Jews. Advocates represent the majority of legal practitioners. Other practitioners include *Wakils* who are specialist pleaders restricted to personal status and some land matters. Advocates are addressed as *Maitre* and will be members of a bar association organised along similar lines to the French *barreau* system. Bar associations are regional with equivalent jurisdiction to the regional Courts of Appeal. Instructions should be transferred to an advocate in the area in which the child is believed to be residing. The nationality of the minor determines the applicable national law for decisions concerning guardianship. A child will take his nationality from his father. Consequently, Moroccan law will be applied.

CUSTODY

Custody is defined under Article 97 of the Personal Code as 'the protection of the child from any injury ... and the provision for its upbringing and safeguarding of its interest'. Custody is a shared parental duty during marriage. If the marriage ends, the mother has priority in claims of custody. Priority then passes to the female relatives with maternal relatives taking precedence over the paternal relatives. If no female is available, the father then has a right to claim. There is no restriction on foreign parents making applications for custody or access.

A person claiming custody must be deemed reliable and capable of carrying out the duties of guardianship. A mother will forfeit custody if she remarries a man who is not a relative in a prohibited degree to the child, but she will recover her right should the subsequent marriage end. She may also lose this right if she relocates to a place that would obstruct the father exercising other forms of guardianship. This prevents a custodial mother from leaving the jurisdiction. However, travel within Morocco is permitted without paternal consent.

DURATION OF CUSTODY

Article 102 rules that custody for boys will end at the age of puberty (9 or 11). For girls, it will end on marriage, but the father has the right, before then, to delegate guardianship to another person, for example, an overnight placement with the mother. However, if this is contrary to the child's interests, the court may rule otherwise. Article 108 limits the period of custody to five years if the female custodian is a non-Muslim unless she is the child's mother and she is safeguarding the child's education in the Muslim faith.

ACCESS

The non-custodial parent is statutorily entitled to access. However, this must be requested. The custodial parent is obliged to take the child to visit his other parent at least once a week. Access can be limited further by court order if it is in the child's interest. Access visits must take place in Morocco. Fathers cannot travel with their children without the mother's consent while she has custody.

CONVENTION LAW AND PROCEDURE

Morocco is not a Convention country save for bilateral arrangements such as that with France.

FOREIGN ORDERS

The Moroccan court may consider orders made in foreign jurisdictions. These should be submitted to the President of the court in the local jurisdiction where the abducting parent is believed to be living. The order must be accompanied by evidence of service, confirmation that the order is final and no appeal is pending, and an official arabic translation of the judgment.

CONTACTS

CENTRAL AUTHORITY

Ministry of Justice
Rue Beyraut
Rabat
Morocco
Tel: (212) 73 0709
Fax: (212) 73 2941

New Zealand

- *CONVENTIONS*

  Hague – Effective date: 1 August 1991

DOMESTIC LAW

New Zealand operates a unified common law system. A New Zealand lawyer may practice as a 'barrister and solicitor' or as a 'barrister sole'. A barrister and solicitor may be instructed by the client and has rights of audience in all courts. A barrister sole has equivalent rights of audience but must be instructed by a solicitor. Barristers sole can be approached by a client and arrange an instructing solicitor if the client does not have one. In the context of Hague applications, the solicitor may be from another jurisdiction. All custody decisions will be taken by the family court which is a division of the district court, ie applications will go to the district civil court but will be heard by a family court judge. The family court has jurisdiction to hear family and matrimonial property cases save where prior or continuing proceedings involving the child have occurred in the High Court. All hearings are heard in camera and publication of proceedings except in law reports is strictly prohibited.

CUSTODY

The Guardianship Act 1968 places the concept of natural guardianship, ie parental rights and responsibilities, on a statutory footing. Parents, married or not, will automatically have joint custody of their child which under the 1968 Act is described as the right to possess and care for the child. A presumption of paternity will be raised if a couple are married or cohabiting at the time of the child's birth. If there is a failure to meet either condition, custody will be exercised by the mother alone. This may be remedied by establishing paternity via an application to the High Court for a declaration of paternity or to the family court for a declaration of guardianship. Where parents cannot agree on an aspect of guardianship, they may apply to the family court for resolution.

When married parents seeking dissolution of their marriage or non-cohabiting couples apply to court to settle custody and access matters, the Registrar of the family court is obliged to refer the parties for counselling to attempt reconciliation or conciliation. Counselling is also available to married couples who are unable to agree issues of custody and access which are not attached to dissolution proceedings. Any sessions that occur do so in confidence and are free. Lawyers also have a duty to inform their clients of these facilities and promote these objectives.

The family court will issue interim or permanent custody/access orders if children under the age of 16 are involved. The special circumstances of an older child may also compel the court to grant an order. Unless an order stipulates otherwise, it will expire on the child's 16th birthday. In reaching a decision, the court will give first and paramount consideration to the child's welfare; primary factors being the child's current and future needs, their character, present circumstances and each parent's competence to meet those requirements. A parent's conduct will be an issue only if it can be shown to have had an adverse influence on the child. The court is obliged to hear the wishes of a child of sufficient age and ability to express them. Where custody and access matters are disputed, the child will be separately represented and their views will be expressed through their lawyer. It is also common practice for a psychologist to prepare a report.

Before a hearing takes place, a mediation conference must be arranged. This is chaired by the family judge and attended by the parties and their legal representatives with the intention of identifying areas of dispute and achieving resolution. If the parties consent, the judge is authorised to make any of the orders applied for at the conclusion of the conference. If proceedings continue to a full hearing, it is in the court's discretion to request an expert and or social worker's report and take account of any relevant evidence regardless of rules of admissibility. The court may, if it sees fit, appoint a barrister or solicitor to separately represent the child.

PARENTAL AGREEMENTS

The family court will give full effect to arrangements mutually agreed by parents regarding the custody, access and upbringing of their children, save where enforcement is not considered to be in the child's best interests. If agreements are negotiated during the course of litigation, they will usually be recorded as consent orders. A formal agreement drawn up by a lawyer in another jurisdiction, will be recognised and enforced in Hague Convention applications. This may be useful for deciding habitual residence or for future disputes concerning the care of the child.

WARDSHIP

Wardship places the child under the guardianship of the High Court. It is regarded as a remedy of last resort intended to maintain the status quo and promote the swift resolution of custodial dispute. In the context of abduction, its use may be appropriate where the child is about to be removed from the jurisdiction or it is believed that the child is being kept in hiding within New Zealand. It is not common practice to seek this remedy. An order preventing removal is regarded as the more popular alternative. The exercise of wardship can be for a general or particular purpose and the court usually delegates day-to-day authority to an agent. Although, wardship gives the court an overriding authority, it is not intended to extinguish a parent's natural rights of guardianship. A person failing to comply with the terms of wardship can be committed for contempt of court. Parents and near relatives may apply to the High Court, but applications from other persons will require leave of the court. Once the child reaches the age of 18, the court's powers become limited, but the child will remain a ward until the order is discharged or reaches the age of 20 or marries.

GUARDIANSHIP OF THE FAMILY COURT

This remedy operates on similar lines to wardship where no suitable persons can be appointed guardian. It gives the family court the same rights over the child and his property as an ordinary guardian. It is not a continuous order, expiring after 12 months or on the child's twentieth birthday or on marriage, whichever is the earlier.

CONVENTION LAW AND PROCEDURE

The Hague Convention is incorporated into New Zealand law by the Guardianship Amendment Act 1991. The Central Authority, a department within the Ministry of Justice, will check that Convention criteria are satisfied and accompanying documentation is correct. Once accepted, the application is forwarded to the family court located in the area in which the abducted child is living.

When investigation of the child's and/or the abductor's whereabouts is required, the Central Authority will approach New Zealand Interpol and/or the police for assistance, for example, in checking flight arrival information. Due to the relatively small size of New Zealand's population, investigation procedures are informal, but recent privacy legislation may soon put a stop to this practice making specific legislation on disclosure necessary in future. The Central Authority will also contact a lawyer in the area in which the child is believed to be residing. Usually, the Central Authority will forward papers requesting return to the lawyer (copies) and appropriate court (originals) simultaneously.

The family court will appoint a 'barrister and solicitor' or a 'barrister' on the applicant's behalf ensuring that the applicant is represented by senior counsel who is experienced in Convention cases. In practice, the Central Authority operates an informal panel of lawyers known to have expertise in Hague proceedings whom the Central Authority approaches on a case by case basis. Once availability is confirmed, the Central Authority 'suggests' that the family court appoints a particular lawyer to represent the applicant.

The lawyer will contact the applicant or his legal representative in the 'home' jurisdiction to confirm instructions. At this stage, the court will give priority to Convention applications and the initial hearing will follow a few days after proceedings are filed making a request for return under the Guardian Amendment Act 1991. The lawyer will also seek any necessary interim direction by filing ex parte applications for an order preventing the child's removal from the country, directions for an urgent pre-trial conference and an urgent hearing and reduction in the time allowed for filing a defence from 21 days to 72 hours. Once filing has occurred, the family court judge will consider the application on the same day and usually interim orders will be made without difficulty. The abductor will be served immediately and the lawyer is able to open negotiations for voluntary return. Negotiations can continue until the beginning of a hearing.

The pre-trail conference will follow the initial hearing by a few days. This will determine issues in dispute and further directions will be made in relation to the filing of affidavits. A final hearing date will be set which will be between four and six weeks of the pre-trial conference. The speed of remaining proceedings will be influenced by the court's case-load and the circumstances of the case. For example, an instance where the abductor is isolated and known to be a non-custodial parent would be regarded as far more urgent than a case involving an abductor who is the primary carer with easy access to family support and welfare benefits. The chief family court judge is notified of every application filed and judicial policy adheres to the principle of speedy process and hearing of Hague applications. Consequently, it is rare for a final hearing not to be disposed of within six weeks of the filing of the first application. It is not necessary for an applicant to attend, but the respondent will be required to do so and will be given at least three weeks notice. This said, some cross-examination of evidence is possible and an applicant may be well advised to attend.

There is a right of appeal from the family court to the High Court, and a further appeal may be made to the Court of Appeal located in Wellington. In theory, appeals are rehearings of the facts. In practice, appeals are generally more tightly defined hearings as the court does not permit a full rehearing of the evidence and law. Enforcement of the original order will be delayed only if the applicant seeks a formal stay of the family court order from the court originating the order. Applications to stay enforcement are rarely refused, but the application must be made and formalities observed.

DEFENCES

ARTICLE 12

There is no presumption of settlement if an application is made after 12 months. The burden rests with the respondent to demonstrate that the child has more than merely adjusted to his new surroundings but has fully settled into all aspects of his new environment. This will entail a full consideration of 'place, home, school, friends and opportunities'.

ARTICLE 13(a)

Consent or acquiescence is construed by express words or conduct. It cannot be subsequently withdrawn. A parent will not acquiesce unless aware of his or her rights against the other parent. However, it is not conditional on having knowledge of the Convention but that the removal or retention was unlawful. Delay in applying for return may lead to an inference of acquiescence. This can be rebutted by showing that delay was reasonable and justifiable under the circumstances, for example where one party was relying on the other party's assurances to return.

ARTICLE 13(b)

The court must be satisfied that physical or psychological harm of a severe and substantial nature will occur by the child's return to habitual residence rather than return to the care of the applicant parent. It will be assumed that the country of return has adequate resources to safeguard the child's welfare. The risk of harm occurring must be shown to be substantial, meaning more than an unacceptable risk.

ARTICLE 13(c)

Objections must be more than an expression of the child's preference but an emphatic reluctance which makes the return unacceptable to the child. Objections must be shown to be valid before the court will refuse a return. There is no recognised age limit at which children are expected to give an opinion. For any chance of success the child would have to be at least nine years old. Maturity will depend on the facts. Age is not the sole factor in assessing whether the child in question has a sufficient level of maturity and it is within the court's discretion to decide what weight the child's objections should be given. The court will appoint a psychologist to prepare a detailed report on the child's objection and assess their maturity. If the child has clearly been influenced by the abductor or a third party, this will minimise the validity of the child's views.

In New Zealand, current practice is to have the child separately represented where custody and access issues are in dispute. This practice has been carried over to Hague proceedings where Article 13(b) and (c) defences are raised, although there is some doubt about jurisdiction for such an appointment. Where proceedings are brought seeking the return of a child abducted into New Zealand from a non-contracting state, the family court will give due regard to the principles behind the Convention. However, an obligation to give first and paramount consideration to the child's welfare will remain.

COSTS AND LEGAL AID

All return applications will be automatically paid for by New Zealand legal aid, but the cost of repatriating the child may have to be borne by the applicant parent. However, the court can and frequently does order costs of return to be met by the abducting parent. Legal aid provision for access applications is not automatic. Current policy is for the Central Authority to suggest to the appropriate family court to appoint a 'solicitor and barrister' or 'barrister' to attempt the negotiation of access arrangements. A sum of NZ$500 (or three hours' work) is allowed for this. If this procedure is not successful, the applicant parent must resort to domestic legislation and apply for an access order under the Guardianship Act 1968.

FOREIGN ORDERS

Foreign orders relating to custody will be recognised and enforced if they are registered by filing a certified copy at the family court in the locality of the child's residence. The New Zealand courts will not seek to vary or discharge such an order unless the parties involved agree or there are substantial grounds suggesting its enforcement would not be in the child's best interests. The originating court will be notified with a certified copy of the amended or cancelled order.

REMOVAL FROM THE JURISDICTION

Both the district and High Courts will grant ex parte orders for non removal and order the surrender of tickets and travel documents. Both levels of court have authority to issue warrants to a police officer or social worker to take and place the child in the care of a suitable person until a further order of the court. A parent wishing to take the child abroad must apply to the court for leave to remove. Leave may be conditional, for instance on the making of a financial bond.

PASSPORTS

All New Zealand nationals over the age of 16 must carry a separate passport. Details of younger children may be placed on one or both of their parents passports or contained in their own passport. Where paternity has not been established, consent from the mother is obligatory. Offspring of New Zealanders born overseas will be entitled to nationality and, subsequently, a passport only if their birth is registered via a Consular office before their 22nd birthday. The written consent of one parent is sufficient authorisation for the issue of a child's passport or endorsement of the child's details on a parent's passport. If abduction is threatened, a custody order or specific order must expressly state that a named child must not be removed from the jurisdiction or passports be provided for them. The Department of Internal Affairs must receive notice of the order from the court to make the order effective. Where parents are known to be living apart, the other parent will be told of the application and given 21 days formally to object or consent. Some foreign orders prohibiting passport issue will be given their full effect if registered with the Secretary for Justice.

PORT ALERT

New Zealand operates a system referred to as CAPPS (Customer Automated Passenger Processing System) which effects an alert system preventing a child's removal at the border control of every international airport. The child will be listed on CAPPS until reaching his 16th birthday. An order preventing removal must be obtained from the family court. Applications can be made ex parte and evidence that a person is about to remove the child from New Zealand will be required. Generally, these orders are virtually automatic in the context of a Hague application and the lawyer appointed to represent the applicant parent should ensure this precaution is taken. He will fax the sealed order to Interpol in Wellington together with a request for a CAPPS listing. Discharge of CAPPS prior to its expiry when the child reaches 16 requires a further order varying or discharging the original order and a copy should be sent to Interpol. At the conclusion of Hague proceedings, where return is ordered, discharge of CAPPS should be requested and parents are advised to request a copy of the order, which should also authorise their departure, to avoid difficulties at the airport when they leave.

WARRANT TO TAKE POSSESSION AND DELIVER

A parent seeking enforcement of custody or access rights may apply to the family or district court for an enforcement order and request the issue of a warrant giving a police officer, social worker or other named person authority to take possession of the child and deliver the child to the applicant in accordance with the terms of the order. Such an order may be granted ex parte on the basis of oral evidence. An individual who obstructs the person carrying out the warrant commits an offence and is liable to a fine of up to NZ$400.

CRIMINAL REMEDY

Section 20(3) of the Guardianship Act 1968 makes it an offence, punishable by up to three months' imprisonment or a fine of up to NZ$500, to remove a child from New Zealand contrary to another party's rights or pending the outcome of proceedings to determine rights of custody or access.

CONTACTS

There is no organisation in New Zealand which deals specifically with abduction. Due to the strict restrictions placed on publicising children cases, the Children's Commissioner may be able to raise the profile on certain issues but will not have any influence on the proceedings.

CENTRAL AUTHORITY

Department for the Courts
Private Box 2750
Wellington
Tel: 64 4 494 8800
Fax: 64 4 494 8820

OTHER AGENCIES

Children's Commissioner
PO Box 12537
Thorndon
Wellington

Passport Office
47 Boulcott Street
PO Box 10 476
Wellington
Tel: 64 4 738 290

Legal Services Board
Level 1, Landcorp House
101 Lambton Quay
PO Box 10 247
Wellington
Tel: 64 4 725 045

New Zealand Law Society
Law Society Building
26 Waring Taylor Street
PO Box 5041
Wellington 1
Tel: 64 4 472 7837
Fax: 64 4 473 7909

Pakistan

■ *CONVENTIONS*
None

DOMESTIC LAW

The system is based on Islam. The constitution of 1973 declares Pakistan an Islamic republic. The country has, since independence from Britain in 1947, steadily reclaimed Islamic doctrine particularly in the sphere of personal status law. Pakistan operates a codified legal system which nevertheless retains many features of English common law due to the adoption of legislation and infrastructure existing at that time. Legal academics have more recently noted a shift in judicial interpretation from an 'Anglo-Mohamedan' position towards a traditional–fundamentalist approach.

GUARDIANSHIP AND CUSTODY

The legal concepts and legislation relating to guardianship and custody have undergone many notable changes since 1947. Ninety five per cent of Pakistan's population are Muslim and these matters continue to be regulated by reference to the minor's (Muslim) personal law which is determined by their father's sectarian affiliation. The predominant Muslim group follows the Hanafi school, but members of the Ithna-Ashari, Shafi and Ismaili sects are also represented in significant numbers throughout the country. Pakistan's non Muslim minorities are Christians, Hindus and Buddhists and are not subject to Muslim personal laws. However, they are entitled to seek remedies under the Guardians and Wards Act 1890.

The father is acknowledged as the child's natural legal guardian over their person and property, with the duty of safeguarding the child's education, discipline and religious upbringing. The mother has first claim to custody, ie the day-to-day care which remains subordinate to the father's supervision as guardian regardless of whether the parents live separately or not. Generally, custody will endure until boys reach the age of seven and girls reach the age of 14 or puberty. Remarriage, an illicit relationship or apostasy by the mother may render her an unfit custodian giving the father or a female relative next claim of custody.

On separation or divorce, these rules are assumed automatically to apply, but either parent is entitled to seek enforcement or an alternative remedy under the Guardians and Wards Act 1890. Applications are made to the guardian court which is part of the local district court jurisdiction. On these occasions, the court must consider the child's interests/welfare, treating them as paramount bearing in mind the child's age, following the presumption that custody and/or guardianship are granted in accordance with the personal law of the minor. Established precedent allows the court to depart from this rule if circumstances indicate that an application would be detrimental to the child's welfare. Consequently, the courts retain some flexibility in this area enabling custody to be extended or guardianship transferred but, due to the importance of safeguarding the child's religious education, the courts are less likely to agree to grant leave to remove the child from the jurisdiction.

WRIT OF HABEAS CORPUS

This is the most appropriate and speedy remedy to seek in the event of an abduction within or into the jurisdiction. Under s 491 of the Criminal Procedure Code a petition for a writ of habeas corpus may be made to the High Court requesting the respondent to produce the named minors before the court at a particular time and date. Consideration will be given to prior events with foreign custody orders carrying evidential weight. Factors such as the child's age and current circumstances, if known, will also be of importance and the final decision will rest on the child's interests alone. If the respondent fails to attend this appointment, the court will authorise the Bailiff of the court to recover the children in question from the respondent. Should the respondent refuse to hand over the children and fail to appear at a subsequent appointment, the case and the respondent's breach of the order will be registered with the local police authority which will be ordered to recover and bring the children in question before the court. Section 491 does not extend the High Court's jurisdiction to decide the merits of the relative rights of the parties on custody and, consequently, once the terms of the writ are satisfied, the court can only order the temporary transfer of custody to the petitioner pending the decision of the guardian court.

It may also be useful for the reader to note that, unlike most Islamic jurisdictions, children are not automatically assumed to be Pakistani nationals, even when both parents are of Pakistani origin but this will not prevent the court from taking jurisdiction. A child may qualify for nationality, but until this is formalised the minor will be considered foreign and require a visa. In the event that a visa has expired, this may serve to strengthen a petition and/or a request to immigration authorities to make inquiries which may assist in locating the child.

THE GUARDIANS AND WARDS ACT 1890

Similar to Indian legal practice, the Guardians and Wards Act 1890 is commonly cited in support of a petition of a writ of habeas corpus. Section 12 authorises the court to make an interlocutory order to produce a minor at a certain time and place and make any temporary custody and protection orders as it thinks fit pending a full hearing. Section 25 of the Act stipulates that where a minor is removed from the custody of his guardian, the court may order the child's return if it is satisfied that it is in the child's interests to do so. Section 25(5) allows for such an order to be made in favour of a natural guardian who is resident outside the jurisdiction or for the appointment of a guardian resident outside the jurisdiction. Section 26 stipulates that a court-appointed guardian may not remove the child from the area of the court's jurisdiction without leave. This legislation remains current throughout the Indian subcontinent countries of Pakistan, India and Bangladesh. However, its interpretation and application in one jurisdiction may be clearly distinct from that in another jurisdiction depending on the prevailing religious doctrines and the extent to which secular theories exercise influence.

ACCESS

This right is recognised and in this context the child's welfare is deemed paramount. Generally, access should be sufficient to allow the guardian to exercise his supervisory function. Instructions should, ideally, be transferred to a recommended advocate known to have experience in child abduction matters. Advocates are governed by the Bar Council Rules and the extent of their rights of audience will depend on the number of years they have been admitted. For the first two years, advocates may represent their clients in court only up to the district court level/lower courts. Thereafter, enrolment may be sought as an 'advocate of the High Court'. After 10 years, subject to approval by the Pakistani Bar Council or Punjab Bar Council, a High Court advocate becomes eligible to practise as an 'Advocate of the Supreme Court' and the rank of 'Senior Advocate of the Supreme Court' may be achieved 10 years after that. The Supreme Court is the final court of appeal, hearing appeals from the Federal Shariat Court and the provincial High Courts. The Federal Shariat Court has authority to set aside legislation held repugnant to Islamic principles and the High Courts and the courts below are bound by these decisions.

CONVENTION LAW AND PROCEDURE

Pakistan is not a Convention country.

FOREIGN ORDERS

Foreign custody orders are not automatically enforceable, by virtue of s 13 of the Code of Civil Procedure. A foreign judgment may serve as a cause of action to file a fresh petition in the guardian court. The higher the level of foreign court, the more weight the foreign order will carry. The court may refuse enforcement on procedural grounds or if it contradicts applicable Pakistani law.

CONTACTS

reunite can offer assistance with provision of overseas contacts.

PART
2

South Africa

- *CONVENTIONS*
  Hague – Effective date: 1 October 1997

DOMESTIC LAW

THE SOUTH AFRICAN LEGAL SYSTEM

Rooted in Roman and Roman–Dutch law and influenced by English law, South African law may be described as a 'mixed' legal system. The legal profession has two branches: attorneys and advocates, whose roles correspond closely with those of English 'solicitors' and 'barristers', respectively. Advocates are admitted into practice by the High Court. They are specialist litigators and may appear in any court, being briefed on behalf of a client by an attorney. Attorneys, on the other hand, have in the past litigated mostly in the magistrates' court. Since 1995, however, it is possible for attorneys who have an LLB degree or who have been in continuous practice for at least three years to apply to the Registrar of the High Court for a certificate entitling them to appear in the High Court (and the Constitutional Court).

In Convention cases, it is an attorney who should receive the initial instructions. Such attorney will then brief an advocate should the need arise. Parents should thus, with the assistance of the Central Authority, identify and instruct an attorney with a specialist practice in family law in the local area (or failing this, the province) in which the child is believed to be held. It is important to note that one of the reservations to which South Africa's accession to the Convention is subject is that South Africa is not bound to assume any of the costs and expenses arising from court proceedings under the Convention in South Africa (including those arising from the participation of legal counsel or advisers), except in so far as such costs are covered by the national system of legal aid. It will therefore be necessary in some cases for parents, with the assistance of the Central Authority, to approach the legal aid officer for the magisterial district concerned in order to obtain such legal aid as is available.

GUARDIANSHIP AND CUSTODY

(For Convention implications see below.)

The South African common law concept of parental power (also called natural guardianship) governs the relationship between parent and minor child. In its broad sense, natural guardianship encompasses the custody of the child, viz the physical presence of the child and his or her day-to-day life, upbringing and education, the administration of the child's property and the power (and duty) to assist the child in the performance of juristic acts and in civil litigation. However, custody can be separated from guardianship (in a narrow sense) and the divorce of the parents frequently leads to a judicial severance of custody from the remaining incidents of the parental power ('residuary guardianship').

In terms of the Guardianship Act 192 of 1993, both parents of a minor child born in wedlock are equal guardians of such child in the absence of a court order to the contrary. 'Guardianship' is not defined in this Act, but it would appear that it is used in the broad sense described above. Parents can act independently of each other in exercising any right or power or carrying out any duty arising from such guardianship, except in respect of a limited range of matters set out in the Act. In the case of a child born out of wedlock, it is the mother who is the natural guardian (and hence the custodian), to the exclusion of the father. Where the unmarried mother is herself a minor, the guardianship (in the narrow sense, excluding custody) of the child vests in the mother's guardian, while the mother has custody of the child. The Natural Fathers of Children Born Out of Wedlock Act 86 of 1997 confirms the biological father's common law right to approach the High Court for an order awarding him access to, or even custody or guardianship of, his extra-marital child. Such an order will only be granted if the court considers this to be in the best interests of the child concerned.

Minority in South Africa ends at the age of 21 years, unless the minor in question marries before this age, thus attaining majority. It is also possible for the High Court, on application, to make an order declaring a person of 18 years or older to be a major. For the purposes of the 'children's rights clause' in the South African Constitution (Act 108 of 1996), however, a 'child' is defined as a person under the age of 18 years.

In the exercise of its inherent jurisdiction as the upper guardian of all minors, the High Court will intervene between parent and child whenever the interests of the child require it to do so. Although these powers can be exercised at any time, High Court orders dealing with custody and guardianship of, and access to, minor children are most frequently made in the context of the divorce of the parents. When parents divorce, it is common that the custody of minor children is awarded to one parent, subject to the access 'rights' of the other parent, with both parents retaining residuary guardianship over such children. South African courts have in the past displayed considerable reluctance to make 'joint custody' orders upon divorce, although there are a few reported cases in which such orders have been granted.

In deciding what order to make in respect of the guardianship or custody of, or access to, minor children, the best interests of the child are paramount and prevail over all other considerations. This paramount consideration in fact applies to all and any orders relating to minor children and is now constitutionally enshrined: the 'children's rights clause' in the South African Constitution provides that 'a child's best interests are of paramount importance in every matter concerning the child'. What is actually in the best interests of a child is obviously a question of fact in each case, requiring the court to consider the physical, moral, emotional and spiritual welfare of the child in question. Although there is no statutory 'checklist' of factors which must be considered by the court, reference may be made to the case of *McCall v McCall* 1994 (3) SA 201 (C) in which a South African court attempted, for the first time, to formulate a comprehensive list of criteria according to which courts should determine, on the facts of each individual case, what custody arrangement or order will best serve the interests of the child or children concerned. One of these criteria is the child's own preference, if the child has the requisite intellectual and emotional maturity to make an intelligent and informed judgment in this regard.

Provision is made in legislation for the involvement of the family advocate in all divorce proceedings in which minor or dependent children are involved, as also in all applications for the variation, suspension or rescission of any order with regard to the custody or guardianship of, or access to, a child made in terms of the Divorce Act. Acting either on his or her own initiative, or at the request of the court or of a party to the proceedings, the family advocate may institute an enquiry and, with the assistance of a family counsellor or counsellors, furnish the court with a report and recommendations on any matter concerning the welfare of the child in question.

ACCESS

If custody of a minor child is awarded to one parent of a child born in wedlock, the non-custodian parent retains the right of reasonable access to the child, the exercise of which may be regulated by order of court or left to the reasonable discretion of the custodian parent. In the past, a frequently granted 'access order' has been to allow the non-custodian parent to have the child with him or her on alternate weekends and alternate school holidays, although there is no hard and fast rule followed by South African courts in this regard.

LEAVING THE JURISDICTION

Under the South African common law, it is the custodian parent who has the right to choose and establish the residence of the child in question. However, whether or not the order giving the one parent custody contains an express restriction on the removal of the child by that parent from the court's jurisdiction, the Guardianship Act prohibits the removal of the child from the Republic by one parent or by a third party without the consent of both parents or, where such consent is refused, the leave of the High Court. In terms of the South African Passports and Travel Documents Act 4 of 1994, if the child is below the age of 18 years, then the consent of both parents is required in order to obtain a passport for such child. A minor who has attained the age of 18 years can obtain a passport without parental consent. A parent who has reasonable grounds to fear that his or her child is going to be abducted by the other parent can apply to the High Court for an interdict prohibiting such abduction. A copy of this interdict should be furnished to the relevant authorities at South African harbours, airports and border posts, as it would appear that such authorities do not routinely check whether a parent leaving South Africa with his or her minor child has the consent of the other parent to remove the child from this country. Only if the authorities have been furnished with a copy of a court order (eg an interdict) prohibiting such removal or with an official letter from the other parent's legal representative stating that such parent has *not* granted consent to the removal, is there any chance that the parent attempting to remove the child will be intercepted and prevented from doing so.

CONVENTION LAW AND PROCEDURE

The Hague Convention on the Civil Aspects of International Child Abduction Act 72 of 1996, which made the Convention part of the domestic law of South Africa, entered into force on 1 October 1997. Certain practical aspects of the implementation of the Convention are regulated by Regulations issued by the Minister of Justice under Act 72 of 1996, which Regulations also took effect on 1 October 1997. In terms of these Regulations, the Central Authority designated for South Africa is the Chief Family Advocate who may delegate or assign any of his or her powers under the Convention to any family advocate appointed in terms of the Mediation in Certain Divorce Matters Act 24 of 1987. There is at least one family advocate at each division of the High Court, usually assisted by a number of family counsellors.

Application is made to the Office of the Chief Family Advocate (the Central Authority). On express reservation to Article 26, South Africa will bear the costs of representation by the family advocate but not by privately instructed lawyers, unless the applicant qualifies for domestic South African legal aid (R5 Schedule (1) of the Enabling Regulations Reg 65 1997).

The Chief Family Advocate has the power to search for a missing child by instructing a tracing agent (Reg 3 Schedule (1) of the Enabling Regulations Reg 65 1997).

The Chief Family Advocate has a wide range of powers to pursue an investigation, including by seeking the imprisonment of anyone who obstructs her in her duty (Reg 4 Schedule (1) of the Enabling Regulations Reg 65 1997).

Proceedings may take place either in English or in Afrikaans. Unusually, South Africa has made a reservation to Article 24 and objects to the use of the French language (one of the two Convention languages) in any application, communication or other document sent to the Central Authority.

As there is no reservation to the 'human rights and fundamental freedoms exception' to a mandatory return, as set out in Article 20 of the Convention, the fundamental human rights entrenched in Chapter 2 of the South African Constitution may play a decisive role in those proceedings where reliance is placed on Article 20. South Africa has ratified the United Nations Convention on the Rights of the Child (1989) and the provisions of this Convention, read together with the unique clause protecting children's rights in the South African Constitution (s 28), will also be likely to have an impact on the approach of South African courts to proceedings under the Hague Convention.

PROCEDURE

At the time of writing, no specific practice directions or rules have been promulgated in respect of the hearing of Hague Convention cases. In their absence, normal procedures for child cases are being followed and all cases thus far have been heard in the High Court.

RIGHTS OF CUSTODY

In respect of married parents, both parents have joint and equal rights, which include the right to determine the place of residence of their child (s 1(2)(c) of the Guardianship Act 1992 of 1993).

On divorce or separation, each parent will retain these rights in the absence of a specific provision to the contrary by the court.

In respect of the children of unmarried parents, South Africa is now governed by the provisions of the Natural Fathers of Children Born out of Wedlock Act 86 of 1997, which gives an unmarried father the right to apply to the High Court for rights of access, guardianship or custody. In the absence of such orders, the mother has sole rights of custody in domestic law. As this Act and the Convention are relatively new to South Africa at the time of writing, there is very little case-law to provide assistance on how the two interrelate in the interpretation of the South African courts.

THE APPROACH OF THE COURTS

At the time of writing, whilst there has been a considerable number of concluded outgoing applications for the return of children to South Africa, the number of incoming cases has been too small for a clear picture to emerge.

In particular, whilst Reg 7(1)(b) of Schedule (1) to the Enabling Regulations Reg 65 1997 appears to suggest that the family advocate may carry out, or deputise to another responsibility for investigating and reporting on the social background, living conditions or other circumstances of a child in Hague Convention cases, and even 'harbour, keep safe and escort' a child, no practical example of this duality of role of the Central Authority or its agent is believed to have come before the court to date. The Regulations would, however, suggest, at least technically, that welfare investigations of Article 13 defences may fall to the family advocate.

CONTACTS

CENTRAL AUTHORITY

Department of Justice
Office of the Family Advocate
Private Bag X81
Pretoria 001
Republic of South Africa
Tel: (27) 12 326 4633
Fax: (27) 12 323 0760

OTHER AGENCIES

Association of Law Societies of the Republic of South Africa
PO Box 36626
Menlo Park
Pretoria 0102
Republic of South Africa
Tel: (27) 12 342 3309
Fax: (27) 12 342 3305

Professor Belinda Van Heerden
Department of Private Law
Private Bag
Rondebusch 7700
Cape Town
Republic of South Africa
Tel: (27) 21 650 3084
Fax: (27) 21 686 2577

Interpol South Africa
Private Bag X308
Pretoria 001
Republic of South Africa
Fax: (27) 12 339 3789/90

Spain

PART

2

- **CONVENTIONS**

  Hague   – Effective date: 1 September 1987
  European – Effective date: 1 August 1986

DOMESTIC LAW

Spain does not operate a uniform legal system. It is a country made up of a number of semi-autonomous States, some of which have their own rules governing aspects of family and child law. That being said, the main laws in this field are contained in the Civil Code (*Código Civil*). Article 9.4 of the Civil Code says that relations between a child and his parents should be governed by the personal law of the child. But if that personal law is uncertain, because the child's nationality is unclear, the law applied should be the law where the child has been habitually resident. Because of this, a Spanish court may find itself considering the law of another country if the nationality of the child is disputed and the child was not habitually resident in Spain.

Spanish solicitors are referred to as *abogados*. They are organised via regional Colleges of Law. They can advise their clients and speak on their behalf in court but, in family law matters, a *procurador* must also be appointed by the client and must be present at court hearings. There are Spanish solicitors who specialise in family and child law and both the Colleges of Law in Madrid and Barcelona operate family law divisions which should be able to provide contacts.

Child custody disputes, within or outside marriage, and separation and divorce proceedings are decided in local civil courts of first instance following the normal rules of civil procedure. There is a right of appeal to the provincial Court of Appeal and a further appeal is available to the Supreme Court in Madrid on points of law only. All family proceedings are heard in private. Spanish courts take an extremely negative view of parents in cases involving children who communicate with the media (this includes publicity outside Spain), unless publicity is required to trace a missing child.

Patria potestas (or parental responsibility) obliges parents, whether married or not, to rear and protect their children and confers the right to exercise custody jointly. If a parent is absent, the other is free to act alone. Daily decisions can be taken by a lone parent who is assumed to have the implied consent of the other. When there is a dispute over the exercise of custody on separation of parents, whether they are married or not, decisions on custody are taken in the courts of first instance by a judge sitting alone. In all circumstances, the court must give primary consideration to the child's interests taking note of prevailing care arrangements, continuity, health and education, etc. The court must also hear the opinions of any child of 12 or over and can consider the opinions of children over the age of seven if the child concerned is sufficiently mature to understand the nature of the proceedings.

Where custody has been granted to one parent only, the parent with whom the child is not living will normally retain the right to exercise *patria potestas* jointly with the parent who has custody, as well as the right to have access to the child, the court being able to order exactly how such access arrangements should operate.

CONVENTION LAW AND PROCEDURE

Applications are taken from other Central Authorities, foreign or Spanish lawyers and parents. The requesting application should be made using the Central Authority's standard form of application and power of attorney. Their completion in Spanish and the provision of any accompanying documents translated into Spanish is strongly advised to save valuable time. An application is accepted once the Central Authority has checked that Convention criteria are satisfied and the documentation is correct. It is then forwarded to the office of the State Legal Department in the district where the abducted child is believed to be living. The case is then allocated to a State Attorney (*Abogado del Estado*) who will file the application in the local civil court of first instance (*Juzgado de Primera Instancia*). The Spanish Central Authority and State Attorneys' offices are staffed by civil servants employed by the State. They will not react well to pressure being exerted by a UK solicitor or parent direct. An applicant may be better served if they appoint (directly or via their UK solicitor) a Spanish solicitor with expertise in international child abduction who can bring the necessary pressure to bear for action or information.

If the child's whereabouts are unknown, a Spanish police investigation, via Interpol, can be launched without a court order. Police in big cities are likely to react more speedily than those in small villages. For example, in Madrid and Barcelona there are police divisions specifically to deal with issues relating to children and women. Once the child is located, the court's involvement is needed, for example to order that the abductor reports each day to the local police with the child or to obtain an 'all ports warning'. The applicant's private solicitor in Spain can contact local police if it is known in which region the child is being held. Private investigators are another option.

New legislation introduced in early 1996 has provided a fast track judicial procedure for disputes involving the protection of minors, allowing, it is hoped, applications to be processed more swiftly than in recent years. The reform is not retrospective and will only benefit applications lodged after 17 February 1996. Within 24 hours of filing, the alleged abductor will be ordered to appear before the court with the child on a date which must be within the next three days. If the abductor fails to attend at this point, any necessary directions regarding the child's welfare may be given pending the outcome of proceedings. These could include care arrangements, surrender of passports or require the abducting parent to report regularly with the child to the police station. The applicant parent and the *Ministerio Fiscal* (Public Prosecutor) will be summoned to attend a further hearing to take place within the following five days. An order will be issued in the two days following this hearing. However, the new law provides that this whole process should not take longer than six weeks, since that is longer than the total of the time for each of the individual steps in the procedure, it follows that little reliance should be placed on time-limits. Bear in mind that much will depend on which local courts or police are involved and how effectively the need for urgent action is put to the authorities.

On appearing in court, the abducting parent must declare either consent to a voluntary return or a wish to enter a defence pursuant to the Convention. If consent is forthcoming, the close of proceedings and return are ordered. If a defence plea is entered, the parties will be given the opportunity to prepare arguments and will be ordered to return within five days for evidence to be heard. Evidence may include expert's reports, and the wishes of children with sufficient understanding of proceedings may be taken into account (with the judge speaking direct to the child if necessary). Evidence must be considered within six days of the hearing and an order made within a further three days. The court has the authority to issue interim orders at any time during proceedings.

Appeals can be made to the provincial Court of Appeal, but the period between the initial judgment and appeal can be considerable. The new law stipulates that a period of no longer than 20 days should pass between lodging an appeal and the appeal decision. It is still too early to know whether this reform is working well and it is expected that much will depend on the regional court involved.

COSTS AND LEGAL AID

Spanish legal aid may be available for non-Spanish parents living in Spain, provided that their monthly income is less than 129,000 ptas (about £600) and they do not own more than one home. However, the Spanish legal aid system has drawbacks. The local College of Law assigns a Spanish solicitor to work on a legal aid case. That solicitor may:

(a) have no experience in international child abduction; and

(b) speak and understand no English.

Neither of these disadvantages necessarily allows a parent to change a legal aid solicitor. Hence, the recommendation that a Spanish solicitor with relevant experience and language capabilities be appointed privately, either by the parent direct or by that parent's UK solicitor. The cost of this depends on whether the Spanish solicitor follows guidelines for charging set down by the local Colleges of Law or charges by the hour. If the solicitor charges by the hour, then fees of 15,000 ptas or 20,000 ptas an hour (plus expenses and VAT) would be usual. There is no reason why a parent, or his UK solicitors, could not negotiate a fixed fee with privately instructed professionals in Spain.

For parents left behind in the UK, the UK legal aid system may permit their UK solicitors to obtain clearance from the UK legal aid board to fund professional advice in Spain.

Apart from the cost of Spanish solicitors, a court official (*procurador*) may also need to be instructed, and parents will need to pay a fee to sign a power of attorney in front of a notary in the UK or in Spain so as to authorise the Spanish legal aid team to act.

PASSPORTS

If a child is featured on its parent's travel documents, that parent may take the child out of Spain. However, if there are Spanish court proceedings involving the child and the court has made orders preventing the child's removal, the court's permission may be needed to take the child out of the country or to obtain documents allowing the child to pass through customs.

CRIMINAL REMEDY

Kidnapping is an offence. However, the retention or removal of the child from the jurisdiction by one parent without the other's consent is not interpreted as an act of kidnap. In 1996, new provisions were added to Spain's Criminal Code (*Código Penal*) making it a misdemeanour punishable by fine to remove children from the care of a person who has rights of custody conferred by the court or not to return a child to that person after a period of contact that has been ordered by the court. Foreign arrest warrants are recognisable and enforceable subject to the existence of reciprocal agreements.

CONTACTS

CENTRAL AUTHORITY

Ministerio de Judicia e Interior
La Dirección General de Codifacación y Cooperación Juridica Internacional
Subdirección General de Cooperación
C/San Bernardo 45
28015 Madrid
Contact: Alfredo Pascual Martinez
Tel: (34) 1 390 23 16
Fax: (34) 1 523 29 19

OTHER AGENCIES

Colegio de Abogados de Barcelona
Mallorca 283
08037 Barcelona
Tel: 3 487 2814
Fax: 3 487 1589

Association of female lawyers and judges
Asociación de Mujeres Juristas-Themis
C/Almagro 28, bajo, dcha
28010 Madrid
Tel: 1 308 4304

Padres de Canaletas (Organisation for fathers)
C/Concilio de Trento 313, 98, despacho 12
08020 Barcelona
Tel: 3 278 0294 (Wed–Thurs, 7pm–9pm local time only).

PART
2

Sweden

- **CONVENTIONS**

  Hague – *Effective date: 1 June 1989*
  European – *Effective date: 1 July 1989*

DOMESTIC LAW

The Swedish Parental Code (*Föräldrabalken*) provides the basis of Swedish parental law in the same way that the Marriage Code (*Äktenskapsbalken*) provides the basis for matrimonial law. There are several commentaries on the Matrimonial Code, although the usable ones are only in Swedish.

The Hague Convention and the European Convention are implemented into a special law, *lag (1989:14) om erkännande och verkställighet av utländskka värdnadsavgöranden m m och om överflyttning av barn,* the so-called *verkställighetsalgen,* which is attached to the Parental Code.

CUSTODY

Parental custody (*vårdnad*) is jointly held by a married couple from the birth of their child until the child reaches the age of 18. Sole custody will automatically rest with the mother of a child born out of wedlock, unless the parents agree otherwise. Unmarried parents may also apply jointly to the court for joint custody; the application will be rejected only if it is obvious that the arrangement is not in the best interests of the child. Consequently, parental custody will not be attained merely by a man formally recognising his illegitimate child nor will it be assumed if he is cohabiting with the mother and the child. An illegitimate child may be legitimated by the father later marrying the mother or when an adoption takes place.

In a divorce case, it is the duty of the court to raise the issue of custody. If the parents are in agreement, the agreement is followed unless it is obviously not in the child's best interests. Nowadays, the court will, in most cases, force through an agreement for joint custody. But if one parent refuses to accept this, the court has to award one of the parents custody, and a welfare report will usually be ordered.

If a child is mature enough, he will be heard, which, in almost all cases, takes place through the social authorities and not in front of the court directly.

Expert evidence can be sought through the social authorities and child psychiatrists or psychologists. The parent with whom the child is not usually living will still retain the right of contact.

FOREIGN ORDERS

Outside of the European Convention, Sweden also has conventions about the acknowledgement of a foreign order with Nordic countries and Switzerland. Otherwise, a Swedish court cannot acknowledge a foreign order and declare it executable except within the procedure of the Hague Convention.

It could also be advisable to have an order or decision from the court of the child's habitual residence stating that the child was habitually resident in that country, that the parent left behind had rights of custody, and that that parent was exercising his rights of custody at the time of the removal/retention, or would have been exercising them if the removal/retention had not taken place, and, finally, that the removal was wrongful (see Article 3 of the Convention).

Sometimes, the Swedish court will institute such an order, but to avoid possible delays, it is useful to request one immediately. However, this should first be discussed with both a Swedish lawyer and a lawyer from the country of the child's habitual residence.

PASSPORTS

The Swedish authorities should not issue a minor's passport unless both parents have authorised it. However, a passport will be issued to a parent with sole custody.

CRIMINAL REMEDY

The removal or retention of a child is a criminal offence and punishable in grave cases with up to four years' imprisonment or a fine.

If a parent wishes to pursue prosecution, applications are made to the police or the public prosecutor.

Swedish Interpol can be involved in a search for a child. It should be noted, however, that the parent should discuss the potential repurcussions of the use of a prosecution application carefully with an attorney.

CONVENTION LAW AND PROCEDURE

The Swedish Central Authority, which is part of the Foreign Ministry, will take a parent's direct application as well as those from the appropriate Central Authority. It is advisable to file the request in English, using, if possible, an English application form. Attached documents should also be translated into English to avoid delay. On its receipt, the application is checked to ensure that it satisfies the Convention criteria. However, to resort to the Swedish law into which both the Hague Convention and the European Convention are implemented, it is not in itself necessary to make any application to the Central Authority according to the two Conventions, or indeed to make use of the Central Authority at all.

The parent of the child who has been wrongfully removed or wrongfully retained in another Convention country may, preferably through a lawyer in the country of the child's habitual residence, contact a Swedish lawyer, who will start the procedure directly at the Administrative Court (*Länsrätten*) in the County in Sweden where the child is staying. However, even if such a procedure is used, it is useful to have the Central Authority involved, for example, for getting evidence about the applicable laws.

When an application arrives at the Foreign Ministry, the Ministry will, if no particular Swedish lawyer is mentioned in the application, contact a suitable lawyer in the district where the child is now staying. It is then up to the Swedish lawyer and his client to discuss whether any negotiations with the other parent should take place before filing the application for return of the child or not. The decision will naturally depend upon the factual circumstances of the case. If it can be assumed that the child is held in Sweden under uncertain or unsatisfactory conditions, it is possible to try to get an order from the administrative county courts that the child should be taken care of immediately by the social authorities pending the decision of the administrative court. Such an order can be delivered even without hearing the other side.

A formal request is quite simple; it should list the parties involved and contain the requirements for a return, as identified by Article 3 of the Hague Concention. Although it is not mandatory, according to the law or other laws of procedure in Sweden, to use a lawyer, it is virtually unavoidable.

COSTS AND LEGAL AID

The parent making the application is entitled to Swedish legal aid under the same conditions as a party living in Sweden. That means, however, that not everyone will receive legal aid. Legal aid will not be granted to someone earning more than SEK 210,000 (as from December 1997, equivalent to approximately US$27,400). There is also a basic fee (minimum SEK 500, approximately US$66) and an additional fee of at least 10 per cent of the lawyer's total fee, that the applicant needs to pay. If the applicant is not entitled to legal aid, there will be no other form of help for payment of a lawyer's fees. The lawyer will charge about SEK 1,200 an hour (equivalent to US$170) exclusive of VAT of 25 per cent. On top of this are costs such as travel expenses and expenditure of time. The application for legal aid is made by the lawyer and should, normally, be enclosed when the application for return is filed with the administrative county court.

It is highly advisable for the parent to attend in person together with his lawyer. If legal aid has been granted, a return journey to Sweden will be paid by the legal aid system, even for a parent living far from Sweden. Also, witnesses can be heard and their expenses will be met by the legal aid system.

Finding an experienced attorney is a priority. The Central Authority and the Swedish Bar Association should be able to give advice, and also the embassy of the country from which the child has been abducted should generally have a list of suitable lawyers. The application and the case are given a docket number. The administrative county court is expected to act promptly. The counterpart will be served with a copy of the request and asked to reply within a short period of time. Usually a hearing date is set up within a couple of weeks.

The court of first instance (*Länsrätten*) will consist of one judge and three laymen; the latter are not judicially educated. Sometimes the court will pronounce a judgment immediately in connection with the oral hearing, which means that in some cases the child can be returned the same day or a few days thereafter.

STAY IN CUSTODY PROCEEDINGS

When a Hague Convention procedure has commenced, the district courts are not allowed to proceed with the case concerning custody of the child. If custody proceedings have already been issued, they should be stayed, and any possible decision by the district court in relation to custody, is deemed to be without significance to the Hague Convention proceedings.

The custody question can be dealt with only after the Hague Convention matter has been resolved. This applies even if the matter is brought all the way to the Supreme Administrative Court.

PART

2

APPEALS

However, the court may also want to reverse its order up to three weeks later, if the application is granted. Even if the order is decided to be effective immediately, the losing party can still appeal the order and ask for a stay of the proceedings, pending the outcome of the appeal. This is filed at the Court of Appeal, or, as the last resort, at the Supreme Administrative Court (*Regeringsrätten*). Clearly, the order also can be appealed if the application is not granted.

The Administrative Court of Appeal is organised on a regional basis and an oral hearing will take place in almost all cases that come before the court. Any order from the court, which is always delivered in writing, will be accompanied by reasoning of the decision. As mentioned before, it is always possible to appeal to the Administrative Court of Appeal. The Supreme Administrative Court, however, itself decides, on the following special rules, if a review dispensation should be given:

–   if it is of importance for guidance in the application of the adjudication that the case is tried by the Supreme Administrative Court;
–   if there are extraordinary grounds such as grounds for a new trial or if the Administrative Court of Appeal has, through an oversight or a gross mistake, delivered an erroneous decision.

CONTACTS

CENTRAL AUTHORITY

Utrikesdepartementet
Rättsenhet 2
Box 16121
103 23 Stockholm
Sweden
Tel: (46) 8 405 10 00
Fax: (46) 8 723 1176

Tunisia

- *CONVENTIONS*
  None

DOMESTIC LAW

The system is based on Islam (see Part 1). Article 1 of the Tunisian Constitution declares Islam as the state religion and the majority of the population are Sunnis following the teachings of the Maliki school. Legal provisions governing 'hidinat' or the guardianship of custody are found in Book IX of the Tunisian Code of Personal Status 1956 under Articles 54 to 67 (later amended by Act 49, 1966 and Act 7, 1981) which are based predominantly on Maliki tradition.

There is a single legal profession of advocates who are addressed as *Maitre*. They have rights of audience at all levels of the court system save the Court of Cassation which has a separate admission procedure, usually after at least 10 years in practice.

There are complex rules determining the national laws to be applied to foreigners when issues of personal status occur. However, if the dispute involves a minor's guardianship, it shall be the minor's nationality which decides the law to be implemented. A child will take his nationality from his father. Conseqently, Tunisian law will prevail. Foreign parents are entitled to apply for custody and access via the Tunisian courts.

CUSTODY

Hadana (or custody) is defined as the care of the child in regard to its custody and arrangements for its upbringing. During the course of a marriage, both parents share the custody of their children. On divorce, custody will be awarded to the mother or father (or a third party) by the court. However, it will be granted in accordance with the child's interests which are its welfare and protection (Article 67). If the mother's right of custody lapses then a list of priority is prescribed by Tunisian law which gives preference to female maternal relatives beginning with the maternal grandmother. Thereafter, the paternal grandmother will have the next claim, followed by the father and then remaining paternal female relatives. A successful claim is usually conditional on a 'unity of faith' between custodian and child.

A person entitled to *hadana* must be of an age 'reliable and capable of undertaking the duties of custody'. A male custodian of a girl must be a relative who is prohibited from marrying by reason of their degree of relationship. Consequently, there are grounds for challenging the appointed custodian's rights. A custodial mother's subsequent marriage may also disqualify her right unless her marriage is to a man who is within the prohibited degree of relationship in respect of the child, or a court rules that it is in the child's interests to remain with the mother.

DURATION OF CUSTODY

Article 67 stipulates that boys shall remain in the care of the custodian up to the age of seven, while girls may remain up to the age of nine when guardianship of custody is superseded by guardianship of education, which is generally supervised by the father. However, Article 67 allows rights of custody to be extended if a court deems it to be in the interests of the child. Where the person with *hadana* is a non-Muslim, custody is restricted to five years of age unless that person is the mother. In all cases, there is the proviso that there must be no risk of the mother influencing the child with a non-Muslim religion and the *hadana* must undertake to ensure that the child is brought up in the Muslim religion.

ACCESS

A parent without custody has the right to visit the child and supervise other forms of guardianship such as education, which run in parallel to custody and the custodian is expected to respect the duties of any other guardian. If the custodian should prevent this undertaking by residing too far away, the right of custody will be lost.

ADOPTION

Tunisia is an exception to the Islamic rule on adoption. The law permits the adoption of children, on prescribed conditions, allowing them the same rights of custody, maintainance and inheritance as natural legitimate children.

CONTACTS

Ministry of Justice
Avenue Bab-benat
1006 Tunis la Kasbah
Tel: 216 560 502
Fax: 216 568 106

Turkey

PART

2

- *CONVENTIONS*
  None

DOMESTIC LAW

Although 99 per cent of the Turkish population is Muslim, the Constitution clearly states that Turkey is a secular State. The legal system is based on principles of Roman law and legislation is mostly codified. Contemporary family law springs from the reforms introduced by the Civil Code of 1926. Modelled on the Swiss Civil Code, it removed the influence of traditional religious jurisprudence from the legal process. The Code, and its subsequent amendments, allow judicial interpretation to extend to the consideration of customary law and religious doctrine. However, High Court precedent indicates that the judiciary is vigilant to the requirements of modern society. Parts of Turkish family law continue to bear Islamic characteristics but there are many provisions which are clearly of Western origin. For example, adoption is recognised while polygamy is abolished, and valid marriages and divorces must be conducted following civil procedures. Where Islamic influences prevail, see Part 1.

NATIONALITY

Non-Turkish women automatically obtain Turkish citizenship on marriage and retain this status on divorce. Turkish women are not barred from marrying out of the Muslim religion but if they do so their husbands may acquire nationality only after five years' residence and the fulfillment of prescribed conditions. Children take their nationality from their father. A child registered with the Turkish authorities cannot be removed from the jurisdiction without consent.

CUSTODY

Article 10 of the Constitution confirms that men and women have equal status and this is extended to parental authority (*velayet*) relating to the child's care and property. Articles 262 and 263 of the Civil Code state that parents of legitimate children exercise parental authority jointly, but the father's decision will overrule in the event of a dispute. Legitimacy is conferred on children of married couples, of parents who marry each other after the birth and of couples who cohabit permanently. This last category is due to the high numbers of couples entering religious marriages having failed to follow the civil marriage procedure beforehand. If a parent is absent, the other parent will be entitled to exercise authority alone. Where a child is illegitimate, the court can decide which parent should hold parental authority. Such decisions are likely to arise where a father has formally acknowledged paternity or paternity is confirmed by court order.

The court has an overriding power to remove the child from the care of one or both parents if the child requires physical protection or their development is threatened. In extreme circumstances, parental authority can be removed entirely. On divorce or judicial separation, the presiding judge will allocate parental authority to one parent. Interim orders are available pending the outcome of proceedings which can be lengthy if divorce is not mutually agreed. The determination of parental authority is left to judicial discretion. Generally, parental authority for young children will be given to the mother, and older children will be placed in the care of their father. A parent of the same gender as the child may also be deemed more suitable to exercise parental authority. Consideration is given to the children's welfare and subsequent orders varying parental authority will also be mindful of this principle along with any change in the child's circumstances.

PROCEDURES

Instructions should be transferred to an attorney (*avukalter*) who will advise and represent the client in court. Family issues are under the jurisdiction of the civil courts and applications should be filed at a court of first instance in the province where the child is believed to be residing. A notice to defend will be served on the respondent by registered post. There is a right of appeal to the Court of Cassation. If the whereabouts of the child remain unconfirmed, assistance should be sought from the Ministry of the Interior which has responsibility for the co-ordination of government departments and the police in matters of child abduction. Turkish children cases may continue for a long period before a trial resolution is reached.

LEGAL AID

Legal aid is available for court proceedings. There is no set limit for financial qualification, but applicants must demonstrate a real inability to pay. A certificate or confirmation from an official authority that a named person is in a state of poverty would be sufficient proof. Applicants must also show that their case has merit. Applications are assessed by the competent civil court prior to or during proceedings. Where the applicant has no representation, a lawyer can be appointed for them. Please note that provision will be forthcoming only if the applicant's case is successful. Turkey is a signatory to the European Agreement on the Transmission of Applications for Legal Aid (see p 11).

CONVENTION LAW AND PROCEDURE

Turkey is, at present, a non-Convention country. However, it signed the 1980 Hague Convention in 1998, and ratification is pending. Further, Article 32 of the Statute on International Private Law 1982 confirms that foreign orders will be given evidential weight at the court's discretion.

The Turkish Criminal Code contains provisions on abduction, ie by a stranger contrary to parental consent. However, parental child abduction is not specifically recognised as a criminal offence.

CONTACTS

CENTRAL AUTHORITY

Ministry of Justice
Adalet Bakani
Adalet Bakanligi
06100
Ankara
Tel: 90 312 419 6050
Fax: 90 312 417 3954

UK: England and Wales

■ *CONVENTIONS*

Hague   *– Effective date: 1 August 1986*
European – Effective date: 1 August 1986

DOMESTIC LAW

The custody of children up to the age of 18 in England and Wales is principally governed by the Children Act 1989. There is also a wardship jurisdiction.

CUSTODY

Married parents have joint and equal parental responsibility over a child up to the age of 18. Where parents are unmarried, the mother has sole parental responsibility, unless or until the father acquires an equal grant. This he can do only through a formal agreement with the mother or an order of the court. Legitimisation by subsequent marriage to the mother, or adoption, are other ways of acquiring parental responsibility.

Separated or divorced parents will often seek a residence order which is usually granted where the child is living with one parent as the primary ('residential') carer. The other parent will retain his or her parental responsibility, and may also seek a contact order.

In the wardship jurisdiction, custody (so described) is vested in the court while the child is a ward. The person looking after the child pursuant to wardship orders may be entrusted with that child's care and control.

Authors' note: It is likely that UK law on the acquisition of rights of unmarried fathers may shortly change.

THE LAW

England and Wales is a common law jurisdiction but, whilst the court often looks to this in the exercise of its inherent power, the majority of child cases are principally governed by statute law.

The Children Act 1989 is a comprehensive statute which takes as its central tenet the paramount welfare interest of the child when any relief under it is sought. It provides a 'check-list' of welfare-based considerations which the court must have regard to before making most orders. The Children Act 1989 provides a framework for children cases, whether in divorce or otherwise.

Wardship is primarily based on the inherent jurisdiction of the High Court. A child may be made a ward by any person with a sufficient interest, and is thereupon placed in the custody of the court, which then determines any issues which may arise. Wardship is usually applied for only when Children Act 1989 orders would be insufficient. Examples include where a special (eg medical) problem has to be resolved, or where a child has been removed to a non-Convention country, or such a removal is anticipated.

The Family Law Act 1986 deals primarily with the enforceability of orders and powers within the UK (see Scotland and Northern Ireland), and the jurisdiction of the English court in respect of children in an international context. The court may assume a jurisdiction where, at the commencement of proceedings, the child concerned is habitually resident or actually present in England and Wales. In addition, a residual power to permit wardship proceedings of an English child who meets neither of these criteria is very sparingly used.

Where there is an international dispute over jurisdiction, in a case in respect of which the Conventions are not applicable, the English High Court will resolve whether the issues should be restored by the English court or by the appropriate foreign tribunal. Classical principles of *forum conveniens* are outweighed by what is in the best interest of the child. The English court, will in an appropriate case, stay its own jurisdiction, or restrain the parties from litigating abroad. When a child has left England and Wales permanently, and by regular means, the English court will not normally retain a jurisdiction over that child for more than 12 months, if at all.

THE COURTS

Children cases are dealt with at first instance at three levels of court.

The lowest is the family proceedings court where decisions are made by a panel of specially trained and selected, but legally unqualified, magistrates assisted by a legally qualified clerk. Sometimes, a legally qualified stipendiary magistrate may sit in these courts. There is no divorce jurisdiction at this level. Family proceedings courts are located in all major towns, and some lesser communities throughout England and Wales.

The next level of court is the county court in which decisions are made by a legally qualified district judge or circuit judge who has usually practised as a barrister or solicitor. There is a divorce jurisdiction at this level. There are county courts in nearly all major towns in England and Wales.

PART 2

The highest level of court is the Family Division of the High Court in which some decisions are made by district judges, but major decisions are made by High Court judges who are specialist family judges, all of whom, at present, were formerly barristers. Sometimes, circuit judges are licensed to sit as High Court judges. The High Court judges sit principally at the Royal Court of Justice in central London, but also travel to sit periodically in major cities elsewhere. Circuit judges maintain a parallel High Court jurisdiction in a considerable number of county courts, trying cases which do not require hearing by a full High Court judge. There is a selective divorce jurisdiction in the High Court, and an exclusive jurisdiction in wardship.

Cases with an international aspect are sometimes considered in the county court but are most appropriately heard in the High Court.

HEARINGS

Whilst hearings are notionally adversarial rather than inquisitorial, a combative or hostile approach is not usual in children cases and will be actively discouraged by the court if it occurs in either written material or in oral presentation. The welfare interest of the child concerned is paramount in any hearing, as distinct from making moral judgements about the actions of parents. The judge will often take an active role in controlling and restricting submissions or evidence which in character, lack of practicality, or content detract from this focus. Full disclosure of any relevant material, even if it is against the child's interest, is usually expected of parties in Children Act 1989 or wardship proceedings. Oral evidence remains important, with cross-examination possible and usual on contentious issues of fact. Witnesses, including the parties, are normally compellable. However, written evidence in the form of affidavits or statements in advance is relied upon to a considerable extent in children's cases. The majority of children's cases are heard 'in chambers', that is, with parties and their lawyers present, but with no access to the public. Confidentiality is protected, extending to court documents and welfare reports, and publicity is actively discouraged.

REPRESENTATION

Barristers and solicitors have a right to appear in the family proceedings court and the county court in all matters. In the High Court, barristers and suitably licensed solicitors have a right to appear in all matters, and solicitors in all matters in chambers. Because nearly all children cases are heard in chambers, this makes little difference. Nevertheless, the majority of cases before the High Court judges are presented by barristers. A solicitor may be instructed directly by a parent or other lay client; a barrister is usually instructed for specialist advisory or advocacy skills by a solicitor. There are many barristers and solicitors who specialise in child cases, and some who specialise in international child work, including abductions. Representation is encouraged by the court, especially in international cases, and facilitated by the legal aid scheme. However, litigants who, from circumstances or preference, do not have representation, are permitted to appear in person, and are assisted by the judge at the hearing in presenting their case.

Children are sometimes represented in Children Act 1989 and wardship proceedings in which they are concerned. This may be by a private guardian ad litem or, usually in the High Court, by the Official Solicitor. Older, and more mature, children may, with the leave of the court, be represented without a guardian. If a child is not represented, his views, and other aspects of the case, may be investigated by a court welfare officer who is appointed by and reports to the court. Save in public law care proceedings, the leave of the court is normally required before a child can become party to proceedings, or make an application in his own cause.

REMOVING FROM THE JURISDICTION

The decision of one parent to remove a child from the jurisdiction will usually affect the exercise by the other parent of his or her rights of parental responsibility. A removal without the prior knowledge or consent of the other parent is likely to be wrongful in terms of Article 3 of the Hague Convention. Where a residence order is in effect, it is unlawful for a child to be removed from England and Wales without leave of the court, or prior written agreement of the parents. An exception allows a temporary removal by the parent with a residence order for a maximum of one month, but this is intended to deal with short, uncontentious holidays. A child who is a ward may not be removed from England and Wales without leave of the court. Applications for temporary or permanent leave to remove can be made under the Children Act 1989 or, where appropriate, in wardship. England and Wales is a signatory of both the Hague and European Conventions.

CONVENTION LAW AND PROCEDURE

The Central Authority for England and Wales is the Lord Chancellor's Department, and its functions are performed by the Child Abduction Unit. When it has received a request, it will pass it on to a solicitor on the Children Panel maintained by it for this purpose. That solicitor will then conduct the litigation. There is direct access by the requesting parent to the solicitor conducting the case. A foreign applicant may instruct a solicitor to bring proceedings without approaching the Central Authority as an intermediary.

An originating summons will be issued in the High Court in London under the Child Abduction and Custody Act 1985 which incorporates the Hague and European Conventions into English law.

PREVENTION OF ILLEGAL REMOVAL

Injunctions (or, under the Children Act 1989, prohibited steps orders) can speedily be obtained from courts, and on an ex parte to restrain removals. Restrictions may also be requested by the courts in respect of the issue of UK passports. Provided that there is a 'real and imminent danger' of unlawful removal, a port stop may be put in place, a court order is not required. The port stop lasts for 28 days.

LEGAL AID

In Convention cases, the requesting parent is offered non means-tested legal aid. Costs of repatriation and expenses are not met from public funds.

Convention proceedings take place exclusively in the High Court, are almost always in London, and are always heard by full High Court judges. Thus the judge will have a specialist familiarity with Convention work, and a consistent and informed approach results. The court has and uses wide and effective powers, including, by the use of the Tipstaff, an executive officer of the court, to find missing children and seize passports and travel documents, to secure the position of an abducted child pending a hearing. An ex parte application can be made at any time, including out of court hours over the telephone, to secure emergency relief. Child abduction proceedings are heard speedily, no adjournment may be longer than 21 days and, in theory, a final determination will be made within 42 days although, in complicated cases, it may take longer. Judgments and orders are usually given immediately after the final hearing, although sometimes, again in particularly difficult cases, they may be reserved, usually for 14 days or less.

HEARINGS

Hague and European Convention hearings are usually on written evidence and lawyers' submissions. Sometimes oral evidence is taken and although this is happening more often, it is still in a minority of cases. Hearings are adversarial, but the judge may be actively involved in controlling the length and scope of the hearing.

RIGHTS OF CUSTODY – ARTICLE 3

English practice is to construe rights of custody in the widest sense, and in line with the purposive intent of the Convention. A court will first look at the domestic law of the requesting State, to see if there were rights of custody at the material time. If such rights did not exist in the relevant domestic law, the court may be prepared to consider whether there were de facto rights – for example, actual physical care by a father with no legal standing – which are sufficient to confer rights of custody under the Convention. Cases where rights go beyond the domestic law of the requesting State for this purpose are, however, unusual.

HABITUAL RESIDENCE – ARTICLE 3

English judges consider this to be a question of fact for them, and not for the laws, or the courts of the requesting State, to decide. The habitual residence of a child is drawn from that child's factual circumstances, including physical presence in the requesting State at the material time, and the settled intention of the person(s) with rights of custody. Thus the purpose of an international removal – a holiday on the one hand, emigration on the other, or a long-lasting but essentially temporary purpose in between – is of critical importance, as are the (sometimes contradictory) avowed intentions of the parents. Habitual residence can be lost in an instant, but can be gained only over an 'appreciable time', although this can be weeks rather than months in some cases. English judges have striven to avoid a close or restrictive definition of habitual residence in Convention cases and are reluctant to find that a child who has lost habitual residence in one State is habitually resident nowhere.

CONSENT – ARTICLE 13(a)

This relates to the position before a removal or retention. It usually requires clear and convincing evidence of an unequivocal and informed permission or agreement from the applicant parent, especially where the consent relied upon is oral only in form. The burden of proof is on the defendant parent.

ACQUIESCENCE – ARTICLE 13(a)

The court will first look at the evidence, to see if words or actions (including delay or inaction) from the applicant parent after the removal or retention showed an agreement by him or her to that state of affairs, but will also consider the subjective state of the applicant parent's mind. If he or she did not really agree to the child remaining out of the requesting State, but held off from demanding a return, or even said one would not be sought, because of (for example) a genuine belief that the defendant parent would come back consensually, or because the latter had deceived the former, or because the former had received poor legal advice, and did not know he could use the Convention to seek a return, then, save in exceptional circumstances, an acquiescence case will not be made out. The burden of proof is on the defendant parent.

ARTICLE 13(b) – GRAVE RISK

The Engish court imposes a very high threshold for this defence, which is distinct from the usual and more finely tuned and welfare-sensitive approach in normal public and private law child cases. Clear evidence of a serious, real, and direct physical or psychological risk to the child, in circumstances that are realistically likely to occur in practice between a return and an inter partes hearing in the requesting State, will be required. Great reliance is placed on (and faith entrusted in) the power of the court in the requesting State – for example, by controlling a violent applicant parent – to mitigate the effects of a risk. Professional psychiatric or psychological evidence is sometimes necessary for a grave risk of psychological harm to be made out. The burden of proof is on the defendant parent, but serious allegations, once made, must be answered by the applicant parent.

ARTICLE 13(b) – INTOLERABLE SITUATION

This is treated similarly to grave risk. An 'intolerable' situation has to be so bad that it is not just imperfect, but practically unacceptable. For example, a return to relatively poor quality, but sanitary, safe and inhabitable accommodation pending an inter partes hearing in a requesting State would not be intolerable. Dangerous or insanitary accommodation probably would be. A refusal by an abducting parent to accompany a child back to the requesting State will not normally be allowed, for public policy reasons, to form the basis of an Article 13(b) defence, although conditions must exist for that parent to return to live in acceptable (even if relatively poor) circumstances without risk to his or her personal health, safety, or liberty.

ARTICLE 13 – CHILD'S OBJECTIONS

In England, whilst seen as a protection for children, this part of Article 13 is treated in a manner distinct from the usual and broader approach to childrens' views in other private and public law child cases. The court considers (often with the help of a short interview and report by a Court Welfare Officer) whether the child 'objects' to returning to the requesting

State, and the child's degree of maturity. As to age, no upper or lower limit is set, but it is very unusual for a child of under 8 or 9 to be considered old enough for weight to be attached to his or her objections. It is also unusual for a child of 14 or over to have his or her objections disregarded. The court looks carefully to see whether the child's approach shows he or she has his or her own reasonable appreciation of the factual situation, including the circumstances of a return, and is particularly cautious about children who may have been coached by an abducting parent. Children are almost never seen by the judge in Convention cases, and are not (save in wholly exceptional cases) present in court, or separately represented. The burden of proof is on the defendant parent, but the Court Welfare Officer's report is often strongly persuasive upon the court. If the court has determined that the child does object, and has reached the appropriate age and degree of maturity, it is not automatic that the objection will be determinative – the discretion (see below) may still cause the court to order a return.

DISCRETION

Even if a defendant parent establishes an Article 13 defence, the English court will place a very heavy emphasis on the purposive intent of the Convention when considering the exercise of a discretion not to return. The court will consider at this stage all the circumstances of the case, and no single consideration (specifically including the immediate welfare interests of the child) is neccessarily paramount. The approach is practical, and based on the facts of each individual case, including a contemplation of the likely implications for the child of a return, or a refusal and the likely outcome of litigation thereafter. English judges, whatever their experience of individual international children's cases, for public policy reasons treat all Convention jurisdictions as providing a high and reliable standard of justice and protection for children.

RETURNS

The English court considers that the term 'return ... forthwith' in Article 12 of the Convention binds it to return children very speedily, once a decision has been taken, unless the parties agree otherwise. In many cases, children leave England seven days or less after the hearing. However, where (especially to meet undertakings given by an applicant parent) matters must be put in place in the requesting State, such as accommodation, or funds, or a security against criminal prosecution, the court will apply firm pressure on the parties to delay a return until appropriate steps have been taken. Equally, the court may, in an appropriate case, press the parties to agree that a school term be concluded, or a course of medical treatment completed, before a return takes place. It may be that this is seen by the court as the only basis for a return where Article 13(b) allegations are made. Usually, the court will also wish to ensure that the abducting parent (who is often the parent with de facto custody) returns with the children, and goes to considerable lengths to achieve this.

UNDERTAKINGS

The English jurisdiction makes frequent use of undertakings, which are voluntary promises made formally by parties, or others, to the court. These are given the force of binding orders, and the breach of an undertaking can result in imprisonment for contempt in precisely the same way as would a breach of an order. Undertakings are normally recorded in writing and appear as part of the preamble to orders to which they are attached.

Undertakings (for example to provide accommodation, not to molest, not to prosecute) are very often given in Hague Convention cases to regulate and mitigate the effects of a return until an inter partes hearing in the requesting State, and sometimes to ensure conditions are met which, if not addressed, would render a return impossible. They do not represent, in English eyes, a challenge to the jurisdiction of the requesting State, or a derogation from Convention principles. The English court is often concerned to ensure that the *voluntary but binding* nature and effect of these undertakings is understood and accepted in countries to which children are returned.

NON-CONVENTION COUNTRIES

The English court (and normally the High Court) is prepared to consider applications for the summary return of abducted children to 'appropriate' non-Convention countries. The English court's approach is usually that, where a child has been abducted internationally, it is likely to be in that child's welfare interests (if the application is made quickly) to be restored to the country from which he or she was abducted, for any issues to be resolved there. Thus classical considerations of *forum conveniens* are not normally applied to such child cases, which turn instead on the welfare-based principle set out above, and the individual circumstances of the child concerned. Whilst the English jurisdiction is normally keen to act in comity with foreign jurisdictions in child cases, the term 'appropriate' means, in this context, countries whose approach to the trial and resolution of the problems arising in the case of the abducted child will not be significantly different to that of the English court. Once this test is satisfied, the English court may apply broad Hague Convention principles to an application for a return, and hear the case with speed equivalent to that in a Convention case. However, it is important to note that the child's welfare is paramount in such a non-Convention application, and if welfare considerations do not suggest a summary return is right, even if there is no equivalent of a Hague Convention defence, the court will not order a return. Where a non-Convention summary return order is made, enforcement is similar to that in a Convention case. When a Convention application fails on a technicality, the English High Court may be prepared to consider a non-Convention summary return on the same facts – see Article 18 of the Hague Convention. Non-Convention applications are usually made in wardship, but are sometimes attempted under the Children Act 1989.

AFTER A SUMMARY HEARING

If a summary (Convention or non-Convention) hearing results in a return, the English court, which bases its jurisdiction on a child's habitual residence or physical presence, will not normally seek to maintain an interest. If there is no return, the English court will usually at once assume a substantive jurisdiction to resolve (including if necessary a full investigation into welfare) any issues in respect of the child.

CRIMINAL PROVISIONS

The Child Abduction Act 1984 establishes criminal offences of parental and non-parental child abduction. Non-consensual removals from England and Wales are specifically criminalised (subject to caveats and defences set out in the Act). The maximum penalty is seven years' imprisonment. Prosecutions can be brought only with the consent of the Director of Public Prosecutions and are relatively rare. Dependent on England and Wales' treaty arrangements with other States, applications for extradition for criminal child abduction may be possible, in both incoming and outgoing cases.

CONTACTS

CENTRAL AUTHORITY

Lord Chancellor's Department
Child Abduction Unit
81 Chancery Lane
London WC2A 1DD
Tel: 0171 911 7127
Fax: 0171 311 7248

OTHER AGENCIES

Foreign and Commonwealth Office
Consular Division
1 Palace Street
London SW1E 5HG
Tel: 0171 270 1500

United Kingdom Passport Agency
Clive House
Petty France
London SW1H 9HD
Tel: 0171 271 8629

reunite (See p 28 for address and telephone numbers.)

UK: Guernsey

■ *CONVENTIONS*
  None

DOMESTIC LAW

The jurisdiction or *Bailiwick* of Guernsey also includes the islands of Alderney, Sark, Herme and Jethou, although Sark and Alderney have their own courts. Lawyers are referred to as advocates and they have rights of audience in all courts. Advocates do not exclusively practice in specialised areas of law. The office of the Greffe of the Royal Court responsible for administration of the court system will be able to refer parents to a small group of advocates who are able to offer strong family/child law expertise. Like the other Channel Island jurisdiction of Jersey, there is little written law on abduction, hence some of the information below is based on established practice rather than legislation.

All proceedings take place in the Royal Court Building in Guernsey's capital, St Peter Port, and are heard in camera. Custody decisions on divorce or thereafter will be within the jurisdiction of the Matrimonial Causes Division of the Royal Court. Applications will be heard by the bailiff (who is president of the Royal Court) or the deputy bailiff sitting alone. There is a right of appeal to the Guernsey Court of Appeal.

Disputes involving unmarried parents are settled within the magistrates' court by a magistrate. Married parents are also entitled to use this procedure where a custody order, separate from divorce, is desired. This method is regarded as speedier and less costly. There is a right of appeal to the Matrimonial Causes Division of the Royal Court presided over by the bailiff or deputy bailiff, and a further right of appeal to the Guernsey Court of Appeal.

CUSTODY

Custody legislation is mostly contained in the Guardianship of Minors (Guernsey) Law 1978 and the Domestic Proceedings and Magistrates' Court (Guernsey) Law 1988. Married couples share parental rights and duties jointly, while an unmarried mother will exercise such rights and duties alone. The child's welfare is the court's first and paramount consideration and the claims of one parent are not superior to the claims of the other. Parents may apply for custody and access orders can be sought for any child below 'full age', ie 18. Grandparents may also apply for access, without the court's leave. Custody orders should be applied for under s 7 of the Domestic Proceedings and Magistrates' Court (Guernsey) Law 1988. On divorce or separation, interim orders can be obtained pending the outcome of proceedings. Thereafter, applications can be made seeking variation or discharge. Arrangements mutually agreed by parents will be enforced by the court only if it is in the child's interests to do so. The court can request a written or oral report from a representative of the Children Board on any specified matter if available information is insufficient.

PROHIBITION ON REMOVAL

An order sought under s 25(1) of the Domestic Proceedings and Magistrates' Court (Guernsey) Law 1988 will prevent the removal from the *Bailiwick* of a child under 16. Applications under Article 43A of the Matrimonial Causes Law 1939 may be made ex parte to the Matrimonial Causes Division of the Royal Court during divorce proceedings. Alternatively, an injunction may be sought from the Royal Court sitting as the Ordinary Court. In extreme cases, where it is undesirable to allow a child to remain with an abductor even for a short time, the Children Board should be requested to apply for a 'place of safety' order.

WARDSHIP

Under the Guardianship of Minors (Guernsey) Law 1978, a child can be warded at any time until he or she reaches majority at 18. Applications are made to the Royal Court sitting as the Ordinary Court.

FOREIGN ORDERS

The courts are likely to abide by an order made in another part of the UK, Guernsey's judiciary has routinely recognised and enforced English court orders relating to children in the past and has upheld the principle of comity when dealing with other jurisdictions.

COSTS AND LEGAL AID

Although there is no formal system for legal aid, advocates may provide services pro bono or at a reduced rate. This arrangement is under the auspices of the Greffe of the Royal Court which will assign an advocate to a case after considering the completed application form. If a family lawyer is required, this is taken into account. The appointed advocate can charge for his services, but may agree not to do so, and he may request disbursements based on his assessment of his client's ability to pay.

CONTACTS

Guernsey is not a Convention country, even though it is part of the UK.

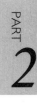

OTHER AGENCIES

The Royal Courts of Justice
Royal Court House
St Peter Port
Guernsey
GY1 2PB
Contact: Bailiff or Deputy Bailiff
Tel: 01481 726 161

HM Greffier (Legal Aid)
The Greffe
Royal Court House
St Peter Port
Guernsey
Tel: 01481 725277
Fax: 01481 715097

HM Procureur (HM Attorney General)
St James' Chambers
St Peter Port
Guernsey
Tel: 01481 723355
Fax: 01481 725439

Children Board
Edward T Wheadon House
Le Truchot
St Peter Port
Guernsey
Tel: 01481 720500
Fax: 01481 714421

reunite (See p 28 for address and telephone numbers.)

UK: Isle of Man

■ *CONVENTIONS*
Hague – *Effective date: 14 October 1991*
European – *Effective date: 14 October 1991*

DOMESTIC LAW

The Family Law Act 1991 of Tynwald incorporates similar provisions to the Children Act 1989 but does not include provisions covering care and supervision orders. Wardship may also be applied for. The majority of custody cases are heard in the High Court of the Isle of Man and proceedings will be brought by an advocate.

LEGAL AID

Provision for applications again follows the practice in the UK, ie automatic non-contributory legal aid for incoming applications with the defended application and contact application being means and merit tested under the Green Form Scheme. Applicants on income support or family credit will be eligible without enquiry. Eligibility for legal aid and assistance under the Green Form Scheme is determined by the clients' resources in the seven days up to and including the date of application. Income between £77 and £147 per week will require a contribution. Legal aid eligibility is assessed on the clients' projected disposable income in the next 12 months from the date of the application. Contributions will be required from those with an income of between £4,000 and £8,000 pa. Emergency legal aid is not available.

CONFLICT OF JURISDICTION

Conflict between UK and Manx jurisdictions is no longer a problem. Under the Child Custody and Abduction 1986 (Isle of Man) Order 1994, SI 1994/2799, Manx orders to stay proceedings will be effective in the UK and vice versa.

CONVENTION LAW AND PROCEDURE

There have been no Hague Convention applications made via the Isle of Man office to date. Although the Isle of Man has its own legislation (the Child Custody Act 1987 of Tynwald), it is safe to assume that Manx rulings will follow existing English case-law. Cases will be allocated by the Central Authority to an advocate (the profession is not split into two branches as it is in the UK), with experience in family law. However, there are no specialist family practitioners on the island. Applications will be heard in the High Court of Justice of the Isle of Man based in Douglas by one of two Deemsters (judges). Appeals are made to the Appeal Division and are heard by the other Deemster sitting with an English QC appointed as a Judge of Appeal.

CONTACTS

CENTRAL AUTHORITY

HM Attorney-General's Chambers
Government Offices
Douglas
Isle of Man
IM1 3PP
Tel: 01624 685 451
Fax: 01624 629 162

OTHER AGENCIES

Isle of Man Law Society
Victoria Chambers
Victoria Street
Douglas
Isle of Man

Legal Aid Board
21a Athol Street
Douglas
Isle of Man
IM1 lLB
Tel: 01624 662910

UK: Jersey

■ *CONVENTIONS*
None

DOMESTIC LAW

Jersey operates a common law system. Jurisdiction covers the island of Jersey only (see 'Guernsey' on p 189 for further information on the Channel Islands). Lawyers are known as advocates with rights of audience in all courts. There are no specialist family lawyers available on the island. The Bailiff of Jersey is the nearest equivalent to the Lord Chancellor's position. Jersey Law's origins lie in old Normandy and English law. There is little published material on Jersey law, with minimal case-law on child custody and abduction. These issues are subject to the court's discretion. However, as a general principle:

(1) matrimonial law does not recognise no fault breakdown of a marriage and the courts still regard conduct as a prerequisite for granting a divorce;

(2) divorce proceedings encompass custody matters. Matrimonial law (despite these features) has taken cognisance of English legislation and English case law can be referred to;

(3) matrimonial law is under review, but reform of child abduction law is unlikely in the near future.

Under common law, a father is presumed to retain custody of a legitimate child. Unless a mother proves grounds for divorce, she is likely to have difficulty in gaining custody of her child and would not automatically be considered the resident parent. In contrast, in respect of an illegitimate child, custody rests with the mother.

All proceedings take place at the Royal Court in St Helier. Cases dealing solely with children will usually be held in chambers. Reporting restrictions are at the court's discretion. Appeals can be made to the Jersey Court of Appeal.

Where children are abducted to Jersey, wardship proceedings for summary return should be issued in Jersey's Royal Court. Where onward flight is feared, an injunction to prevent the abducting parent from leaving Jersey can be sought.

Representations can be made to the court to assist in the location and return of the child. The Jersey court strives for comity where possible. Foreign court orders will be considered. In considering the exercise of its discretion to return, the Jersey court will take account of welfare principles.

LEGAL AID

Legal aid is available for both civil and criminal cases. On admission, every attorney takes an oath 'to help the poor and needy'. Every attorney qualified for less than 15 years will sit on the legal aid list. The legal aid, or *Batonnier's office* decides on an applicant's eligibility and then allocates cases via a strict rota system. However, advocates can transfer cases to colleagues within a firm. Consequently, the larger firms may effectively offer wider legal aid expertise. It is not possible to approach a particular firm prior to making a legal aid application. Hence family law experience cannot be guaranteed. Advocates are entitled to charge clients what they believe their client is able reasonably to afford. The client is free to make an appeal to the *Batonnier's office* who has the discretion to waive charges or set a nominal fee. Applications can be made in person to the *Acting Batonnier* who is available between 8.30 am and 9.30 am every week day and by post (there is also a telephone answering service).

An emergency application by telephone from outside the jurisdiction may be made but full details of financial status and details of the case must be provided.

CONTACTS

Jersey is not a Hague Convention jurisdiction, even though it is a part of the UK.

OTHER AGENCIES

Batonnier's Office
Advocate Robin Morris
Acting Batonnier
St James House
New St James Place
St Helier
Jersey JE4 8WH
Tel: 01534 509593
Fax: 01534 500393

The Jersey Law Society
Duchamel Place
St Heliers
Jersey JE1 3WF
Contact: Hon Secretary, Advocate Le Quesne
Tel: (0)1534 888 666
Fax: (0)1534 888 555

The Childrens' Service
PO Box 142
St Saviour
Jersey JE2 3QS
Tel: (0)1534 509 500

The Royal Courts of Justice
State Building
The Royal Square
St Heliers
Jersey JE1 1DD
Tel: (0)1534 502 000
Fax: (0)1534 502 098

reunite (See p 28 for address and telephone numbers.)

UK: Northern Ireland

- CONVENTIONS

  Hague   – Effective date: 1 August 1986
  European – Effective date: 1 August 1986

The Conventions do not operate between the UK jurisdictions or the Isle of Man. The information below should be read in conjunction with 'England and Wales' at p 178.

DOMESTIC LAW

Solicitors and barristers have equivalent rights of audience to their counterparts in the England and Wales jurisdiction and instructions should be transferred to a solicitor in all instances. Due to the size of Northern Ireland, lawyers do not specialise to the same degree as their UK colleagues. Enquiries with *reunite* or the Law Society of Northern Ireland will accelerate the identification of an experienced child abduction solicitor.

Where Convention procedures are exhausted or irrelevant family disputes are handled by the family courts within the county court system, more complex cases are transferred to the High Courts. The UK is a party to the European Agreement on the Transmission of Legal Aid Applications (see p 11) which may provide financial assistance to parents who have exhausted Convention procedures. The Law Society of Northern Ireland is the transmitting authority and applications are passed to or from the Legal Aid Department (listed below). All applications from abroad are treated in accordance with usual procedures and documents should be forwarded in pursuance of the European Agreement, completed or translated into English. The Legal Aid Department will inform the transmitting authority of any difficulty relating to the application and the decision taken in respect of the application. Where legal aid is not available, fees, disbursements and other costs are akin to charges in England and Wales.

CONVENTION LAW AND PROCEDURE

The Hague and European Conventions are incorporated into UK legislation by the Child Abduction and Custody Act 1985. Applications can be sent directly to Northern Ireland's Central Authority or to the Central Authority for England and Wales who will forward them to Northern Ireland.

Applications are allocated to solicitors who are experienced in Convention cases.

Once a case is allocated, the solicitor will normally contact the applicant direct and take instructions to prepare an affidavit and summons to support an application to the court for a return order. The application is lodged with the High Court of Northern Ireland and the summons and affidavit are served on the respondent by the applicant's solicitor. If the respondent's whereabouts are unknown, an application may be made for a 'Seek and Find Order' compelling a person who has knowledge of the respondent's address to release it to the court.

Following service of the summons and affidavit, the respondent is usually given seven days to file an affidavit in reply. Thereafter the parties will go before a High Court judge for a directions hearing. The aim will be to list the case for full hearing as soon as is practicable. Although children cases are dealt with by the court as a matter of urgency, in reality they may take between four to six weeks before being heard. During this period, the applicant's solicitor will usually negotiate for a voluntary return which will usually be supported by the applicant's 'undertakings' to the court to safeguard the child's welfare and, depending on the circumstances of the case, not to prosecute the abducting parent and to support access pending the outcome of custody proceedings on return. Hearings are conducted following procedures mirroring those followed in the England and Wales jurisdiction. English case-law will also be applicable. As with all UK children cases, proceedings are heard in camera.

Should further orders be necessary, these will be requested at the same time as papers are lodged from the Wardship Office situated in the High Court of Northern Ireland. The Wardship Office is authorised by the Rules of the Supreme Court of the Judicature in Northern Ireland to take whatever action is deemed necessary to safeguard the child's protection and accordingly it is usual for Wardship Office to liaise with the police when raising a port alert. The use of wardship for any reason will have cost implications for the applicant due to legal aid for wardship being means-tested. The Wardship Office will serve the respondent who is usually given seven days to file a reply and affidavit. Thereafter the Office will place the papers before a judge for the issue of appropriate directions and list the case for a hearing.

COSTS AND LEGAL AID

Provision is consistent with the rest of the UK. All incoming return applications automatically qualify for legal aid. Qualification for contact applications and outgoing return applications are subject to means testing of capital and disposable income. Successful applicants will have capital worth no more than £3,000 and up to £6,750 and a disposable annual income of £7,403 or less. Those living on welfare benefits will automatically qualify. Depending on the extent of their disposable income, some claimants may be required to pay a contribution.

ABDUCTION/CUSTODY DISPUTES WITHIN THE UNITED KINGDOM

Under Part 1 of the Family Law Act 1986, residence orders granted within the UK are enforceable. British orders should be registered as soon as possible to facilitate swift enforcement should it become necessary An applicant has a duty to inform the court of proceedings elsewhere in the UK, or any other jurisdiction. If proceedings are discovered, the Northern Irish court will take note and may stay proceedings until the others are concluded.

The Family Law Act 1986 allows a child who is habitually resident in Northern Ireland to be warded in another part of the UK, or the Isle of Man. The automatic restriction of 21 days on the child's removal from the UK will be effective. It applies to all children up to the age of 18.

CUSTODY

Northern Irish legislation is, generally, in harmony with the law operating in the rest of the UK. There is usually a time lapse if legislation is enacted separately and references for legal sources may differ. The Children Order of 1995 introduced in October 1996 has effectively made orders for children equivalent to those available under the English Children Act 1989. In the context of child dispute, there are no significant differences.

WARDSHIP

The wardship jurisdiction is available under the same principle as in English law. Application should made to the Wardship Office for the Care and Protection of Children and the Elderly.

CRIMINAL REMEDY

The Child Abduction (Northern Ireland) Order 1985 reiterates the Child Abduction Act 1984 into Northern Irish legislation, cf 'England and Wales' p 178.

CONTACTS

CENTRAL AUTHORITY

Northern Ireland Court Service
Legal Advisor's Division
Windsor House
5 Bedford Street
Belfast BT2 7LT
Contact: Danielle MacBride
Tel: 01232 328 594
Fax: 01232 439 110

OTHER AGENCIES

Legal Aid Department
The Law Society of Northern Ireland
Bedford House
16–22 Bedford Street
Belfast BT2 7FL
Tel: 01232 246441
Fax: 01232 332 548

Law Society of Northern Ireland
Law Society House
98 Victoria Street
Belfast
Tel: 01232 231614

Northern Ireland Family Bar Association
c/o Bar Library
Royal Courts of Justice
Chichester Street
Belfast BT1 3JP
Tel: 01232 235 111

Royal Courts of Justice
Chicester Street
Belfast BT1 3JP
Tel: 01232 235 111

reunite (See p 28 for address and telephone numbers.)

UK: Scotland

- **CONVENTIONS**
  Hague – *Effective date: 1 October 1986*
  European – *Effective date: 1 October 1986*

The Conventions do not operate between the UK jurisdictions or the Isle of Man.

DOMESTIC LAW

The orders discussed below are more commonly used to prevent abduction. However, they may be of use when an abduction into Scotland from a non-Convention state has occurred or a Convention application has failed. The gradual introduction from 1996 to 1997 of the Children (Scotland) Act 1995 has had a fundamental effect on much of the law relating to custody issues. Some of the common law and statutory remedies existing prior to the Act remain alongside new legislation. This area of law will more closely resemble English law (see p 178). However, it must not be regarded as equivalent to it. A guide to the Act is available from the Scottish Child Law Centre listed under 'Contacts' below).

CONVENTION LAW AND PROCEDURE

The Hague and European Conventions are incorporated into UK legislation by the Child Abduction and Custody Act 1985. Incoming applications from individuals residing outside the UK should be made direct to the Central Authority or via a Scottish solicitor. First contact with the Central Authority is advisable because once an application has been checked and accepted a solicitor who is experienced in Convention applications will be allocated to the case. Applications should be in English; if this is not possible, opt for French. All return and contact application proceedings take place in the Court of Session, in Edinburgh, where advocates and solicitor–advocates have exclusive rights of audience. Their services will be required to represent parties at a hearing. The Court of Session has the power to limit publicity.

After an application is registered with the Central Authority, a petition seeking an order for return under the Hague Convention, accompanied by affidavits and relevant documentary evidence, is presented to the Court of Session which has the power to make any interim order to protect the child or prevent circumstances changing prior to the full hearing. The Court of

Session also has power to order the disclosure of a child's whereabouts. The petition is served giving the respondent (ie the abducting parent) a period of notice of four days for the lodging of a written response to the petition, known as answers. Seven days after the expiry of the period of notice, a first hearing is held prior to which the respondent lodges affidavits and documentary evidence in support of the answers. At this first hearing, the court is required to determine the petition on the basis of the pleadings, affidavits and documentary evidence before it. If this is not possible, it may order further affidavit evidence or, on special cause shown, oral evidence on a particular point. Similar procedures exist for other applications under the Hague Convention, and also for applications under the European Convention.

LEGAL AID

Provision is consistent with the rest of the UK, ie it is automatic for return applications. Application is via a letter signed either by the client or the solicitor confirming that the matter involves a Convention application and the normal legal aid requirements should be dispensed with. This letter must be accompanied by a memorandum signed by the solicitor explaining the nature of the case and the applicant's interest along with a certificate from the Secretary of State stating that the civil legal aid application relates to a Convention application. Clients opposing incoming applications will be means-tested. Both the civil legal aid and the advice and assistance schemes means tests take account of an applicant's disposable capital and income. The financial amounts necessary to qualify differ from year to year (for details contact the Scottish Legal Aid Board listed below).

Emergency certificates are no longer issued in Scotland. However, provision is available for especially urgent work. Scottish practitioners will be aware of these rules which specify that work connected to Convention applications can qualify.

A current legal aid certificate for a custody order will also cover initiating the order's registration to make an outgoing Convention application. For persons without a certificate, help may be given under the advice and assistance scheme which is means-tested.

For parents who have a dispute and who have exhausted Convention procedures, certain other European State legal aid provisions may be available using the European Agreement on the Transmissions of Legal Aid Applications (see p 11). The Scottish Legal Aid Board is the transmitting authority. All applications from abroad are treated in accordance with usual procedures, and documents should be forwarded in pursuance of the

European Agreement, completed or translated into English. The Legal Aid Board will inform the transmitting authority of any difficulty relating to the application and the decision taken in respect of the application.

ABDUCTION/CUSTODY DISPUTES WITHIN THE UNITED KINGDOM

Under Part 1 of the Family Law Act 1986, residence orders granted within the UK are enforceable by way of a petition to the Court of Session. An applicant has a duty to inform the court of proceedings elsewhere in the UK, or any other jurisdiction. If proceedings are discovered, the Scottish court will take note and may halt or 'sist' proceedings until the others are concluded, depending on the jurisdiction involved. Registration is regarded as an administrative procedure which is known to encounter delays; clients are advised to register their orders as soon as they have them.

WARDSHIP

Although it cannot be invoked in Scotland, by merit of s 38 of the Family Law Act 1986, a child who is habitually resident in Scotland may be warded in another part of the UK, or the Isle of Man. The automatic restriction of 21 days on the child's removal from the UK will be effective. It applies to all children up to the age of 18.

CUSTODY

Parents who have married, prior to or after their child's birth, will hold parental responsibility jointly. Parental responsibility for children whose parents remain unmarried will be held by the mother alone unless the father has acquired a court order, under the new Act, or entered into and registered a formal agreement in a prescribed form. It is not necessary to obtain leave of the court to make an application for parental responsibility and interim orders can be granted prior to a full hearing. Parental responsibility generally continues until the child is 16 and attains legal capacity. From 16 to 18, parental obligations are limited to the provision of guidance.

Under s 11(2) of the Children (Scotland) Act 1995, parents and anyone 'claiming an interest in the child' (grandparent, step-parents, etc) may apply, without leave, for the following orders.

RESIDENCE ORDER

This stipulates with whom the child is to live until the age of 16. Residency may be divided between parents or direct terms of contact with the non-resident parent. Parental responsibility will remain joint unless the order expressly deprives one of the parties. An unmarried father will attain parental responsibility if a child is ordered to reside with him.

CONTACT ORDER

This regulates arrangements for personal relations and direct contact between children under the age of 16 and the non-resident parent. An unmarried father may apply for an order without a parental responsibility order but it will not confer these rights. An order will determine the nature and degree of contact as appropriate, therefore contact may be supervised, deferred for a period or divided between different parties. Other conditions may be attached, for example, the contact parent may not remove the child from the jurisdiction or contact may be restricted to a particular area.

SPECIFIC ISSUE ORDER

This concerns the exercise of parental responsibility which obliges the parent to safeguard the health, education and religion, etc of the child. It is unclear how widely the meaning of specific issue will be construed.

INTERDICT

This prohibits the taking of any steps by a parent in fulfilling one or more of their parental responsibilities as specified in the interdict.

PARENTAL RESPONSIBILITY ORDER

This can confer on, or limit, a parent in relation to parental responsibilities or rights.

The court will intervene only in circumstances when an order is deemed to be better than no order. The child's welfare will be the court's paramount consideration. All relevant factors including the child's views will be examined and any decisions must be made in the child's best interests.

A first application can be made either to the Court of Session or to the Sheriff Court. In the Court of Session, there is a right of appeal to the larger division of the court. In the Sheriff Court, an appeal may be taken directly to the

Court of Session or to the Sheriff Principal and, thereafter, to the Court of Session. Interim orders can be granted prior to a full hearing.

Additional orders are available which may be applied for separately or simultaneously with any of the above. These include:

(1) *Order ('Interdict') to prevent the child's removal* from the UK or any part of it, or out of the control of the person in whose custody the child is. It is also possible to interdict an abductor from passing the child into the care of a third party;
(2) *Order to disclose a child's whereabouts.* It is possible for such an order to be made against a third party;
(3) *Order to surrender passports;*
(4) *Order to deliver the child, and to grant search warrants and warrants to open lockfast places.*

FOREIGN ORDERS

In the absence of a recognition and enforcement treaty, the court will normally recognise foreign custody orders. However, enforcement will depend on two conditions:

(1) that the order was granted in a country in which the child was habitually resident; and
(2) that it is in the child's best interests to do so.

It is normally deemed to be in the child's best interests to enforce such an order, unless it can be shown by the person opposing the enforcement that enforcement would cause the child to suffer physical or psychological harm. The Family Law Act 1986 provides for the enforcement of orders between inter-UK jurisdictions and the Isle of Man.

PORT ALERT

When an order to prevent the removal of a child from the UK is made, the police should be requested to raise a 'Port Stop' from all points of departure from the jurisdiction. This has a duration of 28 days. Police may act only if a UK civil order is in force. Under s 36 of the Family Law Act 1986, an order prohibiting the child's removal from the UK jurisdiction, which is made in any of the UK's jurisdictions, will be effective throughout the UK.

CRIMINAL REMEDIES

The Child Abduction Act 1984 makes it an offence for a person connected to a child under the age of 16 to take, send or cause the child to accompany a third party out of the UK without the appropriate consent (this may mean consent from the court to remove) and where there is a UK residency order, wardship or an order forbidding the child's removal from the UK also in force. Police assistance cannot be requested without the existence of a civil order (which differs from the position in England and Wales). Under s 7 of the 1984 Act, the police have the power of arrest without a warrant if they reasonably suspect a person is committing or has committed an offence. 'Connected persons' are defined as a parent or guardian, a person holding a residence order or a person reasonably believed to be the child's father. Persons are liable to a fine or up to two years' imprisonment if convicted and three months on summary conviction.

Plagium is the offence of stealing a child from an individual who holds parental rights. A parent with joint parental responsibility would not commit an offence. However, it would be possible for a parent who has had parental rights removed or limited to do so.

CONTACTS

CENTRAL AUTHORITY

Scottish Courts Administration
Hayweight House
23 Lauriston Street
Edinburgh EH3 9DQ
Tel: 44–131 229 9200
Fax: 44–131 221 6894

OTHER AGENCIES

Scottish Child Law Centre
Cranston House
108 Argyle Street
Glasgow G2 8BH
Tel: 44–141 226 3045
Advice: 44–141 226 3737

The Scottish Legal Aid Board
44 Drumsheugh Gardens
Edinburgh EH3 7YR
Tel: 44–131 226 7061
Fax: 44–131 220 4879

Faculty of Advocates
Advocates Library
Parliament House
Edinburgh EH1 1RF
Tel: 44–131 226 5071
Fax: 44–131 225 3642

Law Society of Scotland
26 Drumsheugh Gardens
Edinburgh EH3 7YR
Tel: 44–131 226 7411
Fax: 44–131 225 2934

Family Mediation in Scotland
127 Rose Lane South
Edinburgh EH2 5BB
Tel: 44–131 220 1610
Fax: 44–131 220 6895

PART

2

United States of America

- *CONVENTIONS*
  Hague – Effective date: 1 July 1988

DOMESTIC LAW

The legal profession is not divided. Lawyers are referred to as attorneys who can both advise a client and represent them in court. Attorneys with experience in abduction cases who are willing to undertake cases at a reduced rate can be contacted through the American Academy of Matrimonial Lawyers (listed below) or via State bar associations where enquiries should be directed to the family law section's child custody committee. The American Bar Association (listed below) will be willing to make the details of the relevant bar association available and again consult the International Child Abduction Attorney Network (ICAAN) list. It is important to note that attorneys can practice only within the State where they hold a licence. Occasionally they hold more than one State licence. If, for any reason, a case moves to another State, a new attorney must be employed. However, it is possible for the original lawyer to seek court permission to act as co-counsel.

CUSTODY

Child custody is normally dealt with by State rather than Federal law and reference should be made to the statute and case-law of the State involved. Hence, there is some disparity between procedure, terminology and legal concepts adopted by each State. Nevertheless, the majority of US jurisdictions have founded their custody laws on the following basic principles. A distinction is drawn between legal and physical custody. Legal custody corresponds to a parent's rights and responsibilities towards their child, until the age of 18, and is automatically vested jointly in married couples. Generally, there will be a presumption of legal custody to unmarried mothers unless there are orders to contradict this or paternity has been established. On divorce, it is common for joint legal custody to continue, but for sole physical custody to be given to the child's primary carer, subject to the other parent's 'visitation' (access). Occasionally, circumstances will permit joint physical custody. However, even in such a case, more time will be spent under the care of one parent than the other. In litigated cases, the courts are sometimes permitted to order joint custody in the face of a parent's objections. Proceedings for orders referred to as custody decrees are begun by filing a petition and pleadings at the appropriate State court. Parents may be obliged to participate in compulsory mediation prior to a decision on custody and there may be pressure for joint custody in these sessions. Court practice differs on whether recommendations from mediators or other private or court personnel are accepted where the parents do not reach agreement. Children hearings take place in open court. A hearing will be in camera only where exceptional circumstances prevail.

CIVIL REMEDIES

The Uniform Child Custody Jurisdiction Act (UCCJA) and the Parental Kidnapping Prevention Act (PKPA) provide mechanisms to prevent parents from forum shopping between States for more favourable custody laws, thereby discouraging abduction and relitigation. The PKPA is a Federal law requiring states to enforce, without modification, custody orders from sister States. The UCCJA is legislation adopted by all US States, although many have done so in a modified form. Consequently, it is vital that the State statute is checked. The UCCJA introduces the concept of a child's 'home State', defined to be the State in which the child has been living for six consecutive months with both parents or one parent or a person acting as parent prior to a custody petition. The home State has jurisdiction to decide on initial custody contest. Jurisdiction is extended for another six months if a child has been wrongfully removed. This gives a left parent sufficient time to petition for custody before a new home State is entrenched. Precedent has established the child's home State as the most appropriate jurisdiction to decide custody in the child's best interest. It recognises and ensures the enforcement of existing home State custody orders or decrees and renders non-home State orders invalid. 'Home State' has been broadly interpreted to include jurisdictions beyond the USA. Section 23 of UCCJA, adopted by many States, requires the court to recognise and enforce foreign custody orders 'involving legal institutions similar in nature to custody institutions rendered by appropriate authorities of other nations if reasonable notice and opportunity to be heard were given to all affected persons'. A certified copy of an order should be filed at the relevant State court. An abductor is notified at least 20 days in advance of a hearing; if an abductor's whereabouts are unknown an applicant may request an alternative method of service to a third party. Once registered, law enforcement agencies in some States can take direct action to enforce a foreign order, in California registration can be done ex parte.

The UCCJA can confer an emergency jurisdiction outside a home State if intervention is required for the child's protection and the child is physically within the State or would have been had he not been wrongfully removed.

The Act allows for temporary orders, for example to return a child or bring him or her before the court and has been successfully invoked to safeguard the child's prompt return in both Convention and non-Convention cases.

CONVENTION LAW AND PROCEDURE

A 'memorandum of understanding' has been signed by the US Central Authority and the National Center for Missing and Exploited Children (NCMEC) allowing the NCMEC to process incoming applications. Before processing an application, the NCMEC will first check that it satisfies Convention criteria and that accompanying documentation is correct. If the child's whereabouts are known, the abductor will automatically be informed of the application and the child's voluntary return will be demanded within a stipulated time, usually 14 or 21 days. If it is not appropriate to notify an abductor an applicant will be referred directly to an attorney. On the refusal of the request or the elapse of the time period, the application will be forwarded to the relevant State contact. It is common for contacts to be local bar associations or district attorney's offices who will then refer the applicant to a suitable attorney. Guidance can also be sought from the NCMEC who have excellent contacts with experienced family attorneys. Reference should be made to the ICAAN list when it is available (see 'Costs' below).

The International Child Abduction Remedies Act (ICARA) is a Federal law implementing the Convention. It is binding to both State and Federal law. Applications are civil actions arising from an international treaty. Consequently, the Convention will override other conflicting US laws and hearings can take place in either the Federal or State legal systems. The choice of forum should be made carefully. The majority of cases thus far have been at State court level. These two systems do not merge at the first appellate stage. However, both systems ultimately allow a right to request a discretionary appeal to the US Supreme Court.

Proceedings are begun by a petition to either the Federal district court or State trial court. The rules and procedures followed will depend on the specific State and whether the case was heard in the Federal or State court. To ensure a mandatory return, a petition should be made less than one year after the child's removal. The Central Authority will continue to support the applicant during proceedings by providing assistance to the attorney and forwarding a letter from the State Department to the judge explaining the workings of the Convention before a hearing is under way. Information is provided to courts upon request. It is questionable whether a petition will be successful if filed 12 months after removal, even if the delay is due to inability to locate the child. However, if a 'late' application is made soon after the child's discovery, a court sophisticated in the Convention is likely to opt for a return on the grounds of upholding international public policy, particularly if the application for return and request for assistance in locating the child was sent to the Central Authority less than one year after the child's removal.

DEFENCES

ARTICLE 13(a)

Consent or acquiescence must be unequivocal. Initial correspondence prior to any negotiation with an abductor should declare the left parent's clear opposition to the abduction or retention of the child in order to avoid any inference of acquiescence.

ARTICLE 13(b)

The defence under Article 13(b) can only be established by clear and convincing evidence, although defences under Articles 12, 13(a) and 13(c) merely call for the usual civil standard, proof by a preponderance of evidence. A report from an expert can be ordered by the judge at any time.

ARTICLE 13(c)

A child who has reached an age and degree of maturity to express his opinion will be heard and this may not carry conclusive weight. There is no set age at which the courts must consider a child's objections, but they are more likely to listen to older children. Usually, the child will discuss his objections during a private interview with the judge.

COSTS

There is no national scheme providing financial assistance for legal services and the US has contracted out of Article 26 of the Convention. Some States, notably California, will pay for cases by processing them via the Attorney General's office and ICARA strengthens the Convention by making the abductor responsible for the petitioner's costs unless that would be unjust. Bar associations provide information on legal aid availability and eligibility in their region. In general, costs are high and it is customary for retainers to be paid before work is undertaken, but charges are negotiable and work can be undertaken on a contingency basis. The American Bar Association initiative to identify lawyers willing to work pro bono has recently culminated in the launch of the International Child Abduction Attorney Network (ICAAN), once established it will be administered by the Central Authority, ie NCMEC.

FOREIGN ORDERS

A US court has no power to modify the orders of a foreign court until the original court declines jurisdiction or jurisdiction has been lost due to the fact that:

(1) both parents no longer reside in the original jurisdiction; or
(2) the child has lost all contact with the original jurisdiction for a lengthy period (ie a number of years).

The enforcement of foreign orders requires prior registration with the relevant US court. There is no set time-limit for this, but early registration is advisable to ensure relief. This procedure is also advantageous to a foreign parent encountering continued custody/access problems because:

(1) there is no one-year cut off point similar to the resettlement defence under Article 12 of the Hague Convention;
(2) foreign visitation or access orders are enforceable under UCCJA; and
(3) orders entered by the foreign court with exclusive jurisdiction after the child has left are also entitled to enforcement.

PASSPORTS

Outside the US, the issue of a passport for anyone under the age of 18 can be prevented by making a written request to the relevant US Embassy Consular officer in the country where the child is residing. A copy of a court order giving the requester custody or prohibiting the child's removal must be attached. The request must contain the child's full name, date and place of birth and explain the minor's relationship to the requester. A notice of a request is placed on the child's file. Details are passed to the US State Department to update national records. This will obstruct further applications made in any other jurisdiction. Parents requesting that a passport is refused will be informed in writing of any subsequent applications. If a search reveals that a passport has already been issued, the requester will be notified. The notice is effective until the child reaches the age of 18 or the request is withdrawn. This procedure cannot revoke current passports. Only the US State Department (Office of Citizenship Appeals and Legal Assistance) has this power and requests must be accompanied by a US court order for revocation or an outstanding Federal arrest warrant.

FRONTIER CHECKS/EXIT BANS

The US does not have a comprehensive system. However, a child's removal from the US can be stopped by faxing the airport or airline of departure with the relevant information, for example the child's details, passport number and copies of any court orders. Entry onto the NCIC computer (discussed below), provides US Customs and the Immigration and Naturalization Service with sufficient data at airports and border checkpoints to arrest suspected abductors. However, the success of this procedure would rest on prior warning or an official's lucky hunch.

IMMIGRATION CONSIDERATIONS

The USA maintains a policy of visa entry. Sometimes an abducting parent is ineligible to return to the USA for immigration reasons. Where an application for visa entry has been refused and where an abducting parent seeks to return with the child in a Hague Convention case, a 'significant public benefit parole' scheme has been devised to provide a limited right of entry.

CRIMINAL REMEDIES

The removal of a child from the US or retention outside the US jurisdiction are recognised as criminal offences under the International Parental Kidnapping Crime Act 1993 (IPKCA). However, prosecution does not cover abductions into the US. US policy has directed that the Hague Convention is the preferred remedy and the IPKCA is not intended to supersede it. This does not preclude the FBI and law enforcement agencies assisting in locating a child and/or an abductor. They will co-operate promptly if requested to do so by Interpol (see p 21 for information on this procedure). The FBI can request a warrant for Unlawful Flight to Avoid Prosecution (UFAP) and enter the abductor into the Wanted Person file and the child into the Missing Person file compiled by the National Criminal Information Center (NCIC). Special agents work closely with the NCMEC to coordinate their investigations. A UFAP warrant will permit an FBI investigation and the subsequent arrest of an abductor, who will then be held until extradited. Extradition is generally unavailable in an international context. It does not cover the abducted child. However, if the child is located with the abductor at arrest the FBI will, if requested, pass the child into local authority care until his recovery by the left parent.

Prosecution will depend on State criminal parental kidnapping laws. In many States, an offence is recognised only after a custody order has been made.

Recognition may also depend upon whether the act took place within the State or whether its effects occurred within the State. Close reference to the State criminal statutes will be required. They will also clarify if the offence is classed as a felony or misdemeanour and any prescribed periods of limitation on prosecution. Approximately two-thirds of the US regards abduction as a felony. A felony warrant can be issued nationwide by entry by the local police into the NCIC computer. If an offender leaves the State, FBI help in tracing the offender and the issue of a UFAP warrant is assured. The fact that abduction has misdemeanour status restricts the extent law enforcement services can co-operate and inter-State investigations may not be pursued. (For more information regarding criminal procedure, see *The Investigation and Prosecution of Abduction Guide* produced by The American Prosecutors Research Institute, listed below.)

TRACING MISSING CHILDREN

The US offers a wide menu of tracing services at both Federal and State levels. Contact the NCMEC for further guidance. The main procedures are as follows:

(1) The National Child Search Assistance Act 1990 requires Federal, State and local law enforcement agencies to report any missing child under the age of 18 to the NCIC without delay and provide identifying information. The agency is also required to work closely with the NCMEC for technical assistance and the exchange of information.

(2) Federal Parental Locator Service (FLPS). Under the PKPA, the FLPS is obliged to provide details from official records, in particular an abductor's last known address, to 'an authorised person', for example an FBI agent, or a US attorney, if a UFAP warrant has been filed. A fee may be charged for this service which may vary from State to State. The procedure is lengthy, between two and eight weeks, may not yield up-to-date information, and may not be useful when investigating recent abductions. Requests should be made via the State Parental Locator Service by letter or authorisation form. It is advisable to make the abductor's social security number available.

(3) The Clearinghouse system. 43 State clearinghouses operate as a missing children's registry, to coordinate law enforcement agencies, collect and disseminate information on missing children. Enquire with the NCMEC, with which all clearinghouses work closely, as to whether a clearinghouse exists in a particular State.

(4) State Missing Children's Laws. Many States have empowered law enforcement officers to gain access to or flag a child's official records, such as school, medical and welfare agency records to assist in finding

them. Projects for voluntary fingerprinting programmes and involving schools to identify abducted children have been set up. Again, reference to the State's criminal and civil statutes will establish whether these procedures are available.

CONTACTS

CENTRAL AUTHORITY

Incoming Applications
National Center for Missing and Exploited Children
2101 Wilson Boulevard, Suite 550
Arlington
Virginia, 22201
Contact: International Division
Tel: 703 552 9320
Fax: 703 235 4069
Freephone: UK 1 800 962587

Outgoing Applications
Office of Children's Issues
Room 4811
Overseas Citizens Services
Bureau of Consular Affairs
US Department of State
Washington DC 20520
Tel: 202 647 2688
Fax: 202 647 2835

The National Center for Missing and Exploited Children not only acts as the Central Authority for incoming applications but is the most prominent American organisation dealing with the issue of child abduction. Operating under a congressional mandate its chief concern is the location and recovery of missing children. Services include publicity and a free Hotline for the public to report sightings of missing children as well as general advice and support to parents. It has direct access to national databases namely the Parent Locator service and computer links with US government departments, the FBI, Interpol and some foreign police forces. It can provide referrals to over 30 smaller State (and Canadian) organisations who address the problem of child abduction.

OTHER AGENCIES

ABA Parental Abduction Training and Dissemination Project
Center On Children and The Law
740 15th Street NW
9th Floor
Washington DC 20005-1009
Tel: 202 662 1720
Fax: 202 662 1755

Office of Citizenship Appeals and Legal Assistance
Office of Passport Services
US Department of State
1425K Street NW, Room 300
Washington DC 20520-1705
Tel: 202 955 0231/0377

American Bar Association
750 North Lake Shore Drive
Chicago
Illinois 606601
Tel: 312 988 5245
Fax: 312 988 4664

Office of Passport Policy and Advisory Services
Suite 260
1111 19th Street NW
Washington DC 20522-1705
Tel: 202 955 0377
Fax: 202 955 0230

American Prosecutors Research Institute
National Center for Prosecution for Child Abuse
99 Canal Center Plaza Suite 510
Alexandria
Virginia 22314
Tel: 703 739 0321

Interpol–US
National Central Bureau
Department of Justice
Bicentennial Building
Washington DC 20530
Fax: 202 616 8400

STATE CLEARING HOUSES FOR MISSING CHILDREN

at the date of publication

ALABAMA

Alabama Department of Public Safety
Missing Childrens Bureau
PO BOX 1511
Montogomery AL 36102-1511
Tel: 205 242 4207

ARIZONA

Arizona Department of Public Safety
Intelligence Division
PO BOX 6638
Phoenix AZ 85005-6638
Tel: 602 223 2158

ARKANSAS

Arkansas Office of the Attorney General
Missing Children Services Program Tower Building
Suite 200 323 Center Street
Little Rock AR 72201
Tel: 501 682 1323

CALIFORNIA

California State Department of Justice
Missing/Unidentified Persons
PO BOX 903387
Sacremento CA 94203-3870
Tel: 916 227 3290

COLORADO

Colorado Bureau of Investigation
Crime Information Center
690 Kipling Suite 3000
Denver CO 80215
Tel: 303 239 4251

CONNECTICUT

Connecticut State Police Missing Persons Unit
PO BOX 2794
1111 Country Club Road
Middletown CT 06457
Tel: 203 685 8420

DELAWARE

Delaware State Police
State Bureau of Identification
PO BOX 430
Dover DE 19903
Tel: 302 739 5883

DISTRICT OF COLUMBIA

Metropolitan Police Department
DC Missing Persons/Youth Division
1700 Rhode Island Avenue NE
Washington DC 20018
Tel: 202 576 6771

FLORIDA

Florida Department of Law Enforcement
Missing Children Information Clearing House
PO BOX 1489
Tallahasse FL 32302
Tel: 904 488 5224

GEORGIA

Georgia Bureau of Investigation
Intelligence Unit
PO BOX 370808
Decatur GA 30037-0808
Tel: 404 244 2554

ILLINOIS

Illinois State Police I SEARCH
500 Iles Park Place
Springfield IL 62718-1002
Tel: 217 524 6596

INDIANA

Indiana State Police
309 State Office Building
100 North Senate Avenue
Indianapolis IN 46204-2259
Tel: 317 232 8310

IOWA

Iowa Division of Criminal Investigation
Wallace State Office Building
Des Moines IA 50319
Tel: 515 281 7958

KANSAS

Kansas Bureau of Investigation
Special Services Division
1620 SW Tyler Street
Topeka KS 66612
Tel: 913 296 8200

KENTUCKY

Kentucky State Police Missing Child Information Centre
1240 Airport Road
Frankfort KY 40601
Tel: 502 277 8799

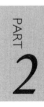

PART

2

LOUISIANA

Louisiana Clearing House for Missing and Exploited Children Department of Health and Human Resources
PO BOX 3318
Baton Rouge LA 70821
Tel: 504 342 4011

MAINE

Maine State Police
Criminal Investigation Division
36 Hospital Street
Augusta ME 04333
Tel: 800 452 4664

MARYLAND

Maryland Centre for Missing Children
Maryland State Police
1201 Reisterstown Road
Pikesville MD 21208-3899
Tel: 410 290 0780

MASSACHUSETTS

Massachusetts State Police
Missing Persons Unit
West Grove Street
Middleboro MA 02346
Tel: 800 447 5269

MICHIGAN

Michigan State Police
Special Operation Divisions
Prevention Services Section
714 South Harrison Road
East Lansing MI 48823
Tel: 517 336 6680

MINNESOTA

Minnesota State Clearing House
Bureau of Criminal Apprehension
1246 University Avenue
St Paul MN 55104
Tel: 612 642 0610

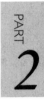

MISSISSIPPI

Mississippi State Highway Patrol
PO BOX 958
Jackson MS 39205
Tel: 601 987 1599

MISSOURI

Division of Drug and Crime Control
Missing Persons
Missouri State Highway Patrol
PO BOX 568
Jefferson City MO 65102
Tel: 314 751 3313

MONTANA

Missing Unidentified Persons Clearing House
Montana Department of Justice
303 North Roberts Street
Helena MT 59620
Tel: 406 444 3817

NEBRASKA

Nebraska State Patrol
Criminal Identification
BOX 94907
Lincoln NE 68509-4907
Tel: 402 4714545

NEVADA

Nevada Office of the Attorney General
Crime Prevention Coordinator
555 E Washington
Suite 3900
Las Vegas NV 89101
Tel: 702 486 3420

NEW HAMPSHIRE

New Hampshire State Police
Troop E
PO BOX 235
West Ossipee NH 03890
Tel: 603 271 1166

NEW JERSEY

New Jersey State Police
Missing Persons Unit
PO BOX 7068
West Trenton NJ 08628
Tel: 609 882 2000 x 2895

NEW MEXICO

Communications Bureau NCIC Section
PO 1628
Santa Fe NM 87504-1628
Tel: 505 827 9187

NEW YORK

New York Division of Criminal Justice Services
Executive Park Tower Stuyvesant Plaza
Albany NY 12203
Tel: 518 457 6326

NORTH CAROLINA

North Carolina Department of Crime Control and Public Safety
116 West Jones Street
Raleight NC 27603-1335
Tel: 919 733 3718

NORTH DAKOTA

North Dakota Clearing House for Missing Children
North Dakota Radio Communications
PO BOX 5511
Bismarck ND 58502-5511

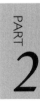

OHIO

Ohio Department of Education Missing Children Program
65 South Front Street
Room 719
Columbus OH 43266-0308
Tel: 614 466 6830

OKLAHOMA

Oklohoma State Bureau of Investigation
Criminal Information Unit
PO BOX 11497 Oklahoma City
OK 73136
Tel: 405 848 6724

OREGON

Oregon State Police
Missing Childrens Clearing House
Public Service Building
Salem OR 97310
Tel: 503 378 3720

PENNSYLVANIA

Pennsylvania State Police
Bureau of Criminal Investigation
1800 Elmerton Avenue
Harrisburg PA 17110
Tel: 717 783 5524

RHODE ISLAND

Rhode Island State Police
311 Danielson Pike
North Scituate RI 02857
Tel: 401 444 1125

SOUTH CAROLINA

Missing Persons Information Center
PO BOX 21398 Columbia SC
29221-1398
Tel: 803 737 9000

SOUTH DAKOTA

Attorney General's Office
500 East Capitol
Pierre SD 57501
Tel: 605 773 3331

TENNESSEE

Tennessee Bureau of Investigation
1148 Foster Ave
Nashville TN 37210
Tel: 615 741 0430

TEXAS

Criminal Intelligence Services
PO BOX 4087
Austin TX 78773-0001
Tel: 512 465 2814

VERMONT

Vermont Department of Public Safety
103 South Main Street
Waterbury VT 05676
Tel: 802 244 8727

VIRGINIA

Virginia State Police Department
PO BOX 27472 Richmond
VA 23261-7472
Tel: 804 674 2026

WASHINGTON

Missing Children Clearing House
Washington State Patrol
PO BOX 2347
Olympia WA 98507-2347
Tel: 360 757 3960

WYOMING

Wyoming Office of the Attorney General
Division of Criminal Investigation
316 West 22nd Street
Cheyenne WY 82002
Tel: 307 777 7537